ORGASM
 for
LiFE

JENNIFER ELIZABETH MASTERS

Orgasm for Life
by Jennifer Elizabeth Masters

Cover and interior design by Lloyd Matthew Thompson

Author photo by Sarah Perkins Photography – Denver, CO

Table of Contents

Acknowledgments

ALTHOUGH WE DON'T LIKE thinking of our parents having sex and pleasure, had mine not done so way back when, I would not be here to write this book. I am grateful to my parents for bringing me into this world, kicking and screaming.

I gratefully thank my friend, William T. Dargin, who conjured up the title for this book. Thank you for all the great support and encouragement of my work and personal growth for the last eight years. I appreciate all the talent and gifts that you have bestowed upon me.

I thank the many who contributed to the Incredible Sex Survey, which made this work so worthwhile. Your candid responses helped to create a more meaningful guide.

I thank all my amazing and loving clients who have

helped me grow and learn through their own experiences and sharing. Thank you for your loving support.

To my daughter, Ariel, who encouraged me while I was buried in the creation of this book. I am grateful to you for your loving support. I apologize in advance for all the future embarrassment when you have to explain, "My mom wrote a SEX book." I appreciate you for your wisdom and patience while I burned one meal after another during the process of writing.

To my sons Adam and David, thank you for your love and support.

I am grateful to the men that have come and gone and those yet to come, for helping me understand who I am and what I am truly here to do.

Run your fingers through my soul
For once, just once feel exactly what I feel,
Believe what I believe,

Perceive what I perceive,
Look, experience, examine
And for once, just once
Truly understand

—Unknown

Women need a reason to have sex.
Men just need a place.
—Billy Crystal

ORGASM

for

LIFE

Preface

FORGET WHAT YOU HAVE ever heard. Forget whatever you have ever been taught. Most of what you have learned thus far has your balls gripped in a vise and twisted. For those of you without testicles, you have spent far too long repenting those you have slept with and regretting the ones you let get away.

Your life is about to change profoundly on a very personal level.

Religion and society have molded, groomed and programmed us to behave a certain way. When we move beyond the middle road of life our palms begin to sweat and our conscience pulls us back from living a life outside the "normal limits" of society. We see a stray sheep every now and then living a life beyond our programming and conditioning. We wonder what it might feel like to not care what society thinks. Our morals and other societal limitations for the extraordinary keep us in check. Instead, we find ourselves skirting middle age and beyond, without ever having touched the thrill of sex standing up in an antique store or other public places. These are only fantasies, hopes or dreams we sometimes read about.

Memories of sex under the Eiffel Tower in Paris and in the first class section of a DC-8, for most "normal" people don't exist. Most of us only dream about outlandish or outrageous behavior that might get us thrown off a public airline. Yet there are those who push the limits, who experience wide-eyed wonder in their lives. We see these players and characters in movies and imagine what life would be like to be them, if only for a moment.

We find ourselves as adults with children and responsibilities that further bog us down, yet create more mundane, but pleasant, events. We love our families but long for the thrill of the stomach-dropping roller coaster ride, minus the vomit, which unbridled free sexual expression can give us.

Life is supposed to be pleasure-filled. We approach middle-age wondering where it is? For all our back-breaking, nose-to-the-grindstone years we have endured, it seems that the pleasure has been wrung out of our sexual experiences. We read about it in books, or watch it on a movie screen. We live in an "On Demand" society. We desire instant gratification. We want mind blowing sex with multiple orgasms that leave us wishing we smoked, so we could experience the post coitus inhalation, then fling ourselves onto our dampened pillows, panting "OH MY GOD!"

Why isn't it happening in your life right now? We confuse pleasure with entertainment. We focus on what we don't have. We think longingly of the guy or girl back in the 80's with the great ass, then wonder why we didn't fuck them right then.

Screw regret. Life is too short to spend half of it wishing wistfully for something we don't have, and the other half wishing we had the guts to do what we didn't do. The more we focus on our regrets, the more regrettable moments we have.

We know that happy people do extraordinary things. Depressed people rarely astound anyone. We live in a rat race of work, errands, then death. Life is over before we know it. Sometimes we see people younger than ourselves dying before their time. I am writing this book to light a firecracker under your ass, to catapult you out of your easy chair, away from your remote. You have the power to consciously create more joy and pleasure in your life rather than watching it pass you by from the sidelines. Life will be over before you know it. Wouldn't you rather have a memory of making love in the ocean off the coast of Bermuda, remembering your life as one that was lived passionately?

Durex Sex Survey 2013

- Over 50% are dissatisfied with their bedroom escapades.
- 80% of women fake orgasm over 50% of the time.
- 26% of women fake it every time.
- 28% of men fake orgasm.
- 35% orgasm every time they have sex.
- 40% of women have some sexual dysfunction.
- 10% of women never have orgasms.
- 37% have also said they hardly ever, or never, "cross the finish line" at the same time as their partner.
- 65% of American adults have gotten hot 'n' heavy in a car. 35% have taken more than a dip in a pool and 31% have bared it all on a beach.
- 65% daydream about making love more often outside of the bedroom.
- According to Luann Brizandine, author of *The Female Brain*, men think of sex every 52 seconds, while women only think of sex an average of once a day.

Chapter One
The Best Orgasm for Your Life

You know "that look" women get when they want sex?
Me neither. —Steve Martin

AN ORGASM IS ABOUT letting go, complete surrender. Gripping the window ledge of life with your finger tips, hanging on for dear life in fear and shame does not get you to the big "O." It might however, get you acid reflux, hypertension, and heart attacks.

We have the best sex when we are "all in." When our mind, body, and soul are completely engrossed and engulfed in the sexual and emotional experience. Great, expansive orgasms are best appreciated and enjoyed with someone that we connect with and love deeply. The best sex we have happens when we are totally in the moment, experiencing the infinite feelings of taste, touch, and pleasure. Our experience is heightened when we are able to relax and let go, shut out the world, totally engrossed in the sexual experience, connected on all levels with your partner. Here is where pleasure, ecstasy, union of mind-body-spirit take sex to a much higher level. It is no wonder we often yell, "Oh God! Oh God! Oh God!" when experiencing intense unbridled pleasure.

When we experience the dissolving of barriers and walls through orgasm, we reach an experience that can only be expressed as an altered state. This is where we experience something greater than we are. Losing control and letting go can take us to a place that feels like we touched something greater than ourselves. A fragment of enlightenment crosses into our consciousness that is unparalleled in intensity or depth of feeling. It is no wonder that men have killed for it, women have died for it: sex is an intensely gratifying and wondrous experience.

The purpose of this book is to help the millions of people worldwide who want to increase intimacy, pleasure and improve their sex lives, but don't know where to begin. Most people want more information so they can understand themselves better, as well as their partner's desires and needs.

Great sex can help a relationship last a lifetime. Statistics show that those relationships which have a strong sexual attraction with deep connected sex are healthier and last longer. People who have sex regularly touch each other more often, enjoying deeper intimacy. Both reinforce the love between a couple. Humans need touch. When we stop having sex, we seldom touch each other. Instead of snuggling at night, we may sleep apart. We are more apt to notice our partner's faults, argue, and complain about our partner's behavior.

Saying YES to sex means saying YES to love, and ultimately more happiness, with greater well-being. Saying NO turns women into bitches, it sends our men out the door to have sex with their co-workers and tennis buddies. There is always someone who will say, YES! Why can't it be YOU?

No matter what your sexual preference is, there is guidance on some level for everyone. Being heterosexual, my focus was directed towards the intricacies of male-female physical challenges and communication. I have respect for all genders and sexual preferences. I have interviewed hundreds of men and women, lesbian, gay, and straight to understand the many challenges and differences between us.

Many women I know stop having sex in their fifties. They have stopped having sex because it was not fulfilling. They didn't have orgasms and their husbands and lovers didn't seem to know. Many felt that their partner's did not care. This is just sad. Many women are disheartened, like I was, about the sex they have had. Just because we have sexual body parts does not mean we know how to make love to another. Or even with ourselves. Many of us need help. Sex can improve as you get older, with some guidance and understanding. Men need education, understanding, and patience with us women. Women, too, need to have better understanding of the male psyche and how it feels to be rejected when we are not in the mood. With new knowledge and understanding more women will be satisfied and happier.

Viagra

Millions of men have talked to their doctor about Viagra. Viagra is a pharmaceutical pill which uses five letters from the word vagina, which I find interesting. This little blue pill was created so that men with difficulties in the cranking department would be able to get hard enough to participate and enjoy penetrative sex.

Men have used the little blue pill to improve their sexual experiences where an erection is challenging or impossible. Of course, there are side effects, the worst of which is death. To think that a man would risk his life to experience coitus is telling. Sex is an important part of life. Completing the sex act is imperative, especially for men. Men have been having orgasms for thousands of years without major issues. Why is it so different today?

Women have suffered from frigidity for thousands of years, with the inability to complete the sex act. If sexual dysfunction was as prevalent in men as it is in women today as well as historically, a little pink pill would have already been created. This little pink pill would change the way millions of women experience sex. This pill would use the word penis to derive its name. This magical pill would be called, Piñata! As you can see, Piñata uses only two letters from the word penis, because women can have almost as much fun without a penis. Like a piñata, once you crack open a woman with an orgasm, she is full of fun, surprises, and lots of sugar. The mystery is solved! When women have orgasms through love-making, they return for more. This is an amazing concept! Instead of women existing in non-orgasmic relationships for twenty, thirty, or forty years, we could be enjoying orgasms! It is up to women to know what they like, and to have partners that will lovingly and patiently get them there before they do.

Given the popularity of *Sex in the City* and *50 Shades of Gray*, the time is ripe for a fun, educational book about sex. Remember *The Joy of Sex*? Written in 1972, it sold over 10 million copies. People want more information, while morals and society have changed.

I am an empowerment and sex coach for women. What I have found is, most people are ignoring the issue because they don't want to hurt their partner's feelings. Sex is a delicate subject. I have a knack for being irreverent and unorthodox, which makes me an excellent candidate for a book about a delicate subject. I take the "ahem," out of sex by demystifying it. I don't sugarcoat it, and I am fearlessly open. Sex, to me, is perfectly natural with nothing to be ashamed of. I also feel that sex has a deeply spiritual component to it. After all, who created sex anyway?

Thankfully, there are strong women on this planet that are heralding a new society, where men and women can become each other's sex slaves, and women are touted for standing with one foot poised on their partner's chests wearing stilettos and doing fist bumps with their "sistas." Oh, wait. That was just a dream I had recently. What was I thinking?

Seriously, to really have the kind of sex you fantasize about, you need to revere your woman and your man. Love, respect and admire who they are. Men, you need to pleasure her until she can't speak. Men, do you want the ultimate orgasm and sexual experience? Then give it up first. Give the best orgasm to your woman first. See how this changes the complexion of your relationship. Women are capable of having multiple orgasms. It just takes most women longer than men expect to have ours. Thinking that we are the same as men is what created the chasm that is currently between men and women today. Most women don't experience an orgasm through vaginal penetration. Yet the majority of the men in the world continue to make love to women in this way. In India, for example, men take care of their own needs without asking if a woman has had an orgasm. It is not discussed. There is not an alternate method to bring a woman to orgasm because sex is for the man's pleasure, not the woman's. To the vast majority of the world, sex is a private, personal matter that is not up for discussion between husband and wife. Whether a woman experiences pleasure or not, rarely enters a marriage discussion. Living in the United States, where we are purported to be advanced technologically, medically and scientifically, most men do not know what it takes, or how to bring a woman to orgasm.

As a healthy, heterosexual female, I have had lots of sex. I have been married and divorced 4 times. During those marriages, sex was an important component in my relationships. It was enjoyable. Sometimes it was very good. However, over time it became flat and cursory. I noticed how truncated, boring, and dull sexual experiences became after years of marriage. We often rush through our encounters because one person is less interested than the other, or when babies arrive on the scene. I hear stories of women telling their husbands, just do it and get it over with! Many women do not participate during sex. They lie still, like dead fish, expecting their men to just pleasure themselves. Who wants sex like that? It isn't good for anyone.

I have experienced a wide variety of sexual

experiences while married and single. A few were more memorable than others. My first multiple orgasm was with a man who was of average size and stature. I mention his size, because many men are under the impression that being well-endowed is the best way to pleasure a woman. That is simply not true. An average sized penis can be more appreciated than a super-sized one. Case in point: my multiple orgasms with an average sized man. I experienced wave after wave of pleasure that went on endlessly. I did not have any of those types of experiences while married. The best sex I ever had was when I was not married. There is something to be said for the excitement of illicit sex. Sex without a contract for it. Once we sign our lives away on the dotted line, it seems we are being sentenced to death: the death of great sex, play, and fun. We have to fight the urge to repeat the same position in the same room, at the same time of day. Sex in marriage can be fun and exciting; we just have to be more innovative.

The Big Death

The French call orgasms, *la petite mort*, due to the way many people lose consciousness or life force directly after orgasm. One of my most traumatic and life-changing sexual experiences was a big death. It is one most women don't want to talk about: the man I loved died right after making love. It was certainly not my intention. He wasn't complaining while we were making love. There was nothing that would have led me to believe anything was amiss. I was in my late 40's, my partner was 52. After telling me he loved me and would never leave me, he did just that. He left me, but he had to die to do it. You could say that is going to extremes to end a relationship. Although in his defense he died a very happy man. All his friends wanted to meet the woman that sent their brother off—literally, with a huge smile on his face. It is the way many men dream of dying. Having a man die during or immediately after doing the horizontal mambo can leave you scarred, afraid of a repeat performance and deeply traumatized. When it is someone you feel a deep connection and love for, it takes years to overcome. Years later, I wrote about my experience in *Odyssey Victim to Victory*. Having a healthy heart and body with regular check-ups is imperative. Blocked arteries and wild sex are not a healthy combination. I recommend blood work yearly. (See additional resources at the back of the book.) You don't want your heart to explode.

In my relationships, I felt unsafe to express my personal needs or requirements to improve the quality and pleasure for myself. Over 80% of the time I did not have orgasms. I had difficulty letting go, trusting, and feeling confident. Being fearful can block orgasm from occurring. The more confidence a woman has, the easier it is for her to let go. Looking back now, I wonder what the heck I was so afraid of. If I had the courage to speak up then, maybe I could have enjoyed life more as well as sex. I found that when I made requests, I sounded like a dictator, which went over like a dominatrix at a Mary Kay convention. I did not know how to voice my feelings without reactivity or emotion. I didn't realize how profoundly my childhood trauma affected me sexually until years later.

Tantra -
Is It True What We Heard About Sting?

After I healed deep and painful issues through Tantra, my sexual experience is now very different. Tantra focuses on the pleasure of the moment and less on the end result. Tantra teaches you to circulate your sexual energy in your body, choosing when you want to release it in orgasm (for men) rather than making orgasm the focus. When men hold and circulate their sexual energy within their body, they are able to make love for much longer periods of time. The benefit for the woman with Tantra is that she has the time needed to raise her sexual energy and reach high levels ecstasy.

Tantra is a style of meditation and ritual which began around the fifth century A.D. in India. The spiritual practice of Tantric sex focuses on enlightenment, reverence for your partner, and the sacredness of sex. It is a slow process of breathing, eye gazing, meditation prior to sex together, and love-making which removes the focus from orgasm. This Eastern tradition teaches that men lose precious life force by allowing themselves to ejaculate every time they have sex. When love-making continues for more than an hour, and the sexual energy is circulated up into the center of the forehead (third eye) a man does not lose precious life force energy. However, when men ejaculate in less than an hour, their sexual energy has not had enough time to circulate through the body, meaning life force is lost. Most men who practice Tantra choose whether to ejaculate or not. They can continue making love for hours with their erection waning and then building again. This is a wonderful way to experience each other and give the woman ample time to reach orgasm. She can have many orgasms this way. For the male counterpart, most want to ejaculate at some point to experience the intensity of this type of orgasm. Often this is once a week or less. It is up to the individual.

The western focus on sex is the end result - orgasm. The recording artist, Sting made a comment to an interviewer 20 years ago, about making love for hours with his wife. Tantra is far more than lasting a long time. Sting has tried to recant his comment in a variety of ways. He now explains it this way, that his wife, Trudy, is his church. Tantra has far more to do with reverence for your partner than longevity in the sexual act. This by itself gives sex the energy of sacredness. Tantra is about giving and receiving, taking turns giving slow pleasure to the other.

When you are receiving pleasure in tantra, you enjoy each moment, allowing yourself to just feel and enjoy the pleasure. Slowing down the process of sex, allows sexual energy to build, and then fall, reach a crescendo and fall again. Taking turns giving to one another in each session could mean sensual massage where one person gives fully without sex. Focusing on the other person's body fully, giving them pleasure can change the way you look at one another outside of the bedroom. Receiving pleasure for an hour, without any thought or concern about giving back to your partner in a session can be incredibly freeing and invigorating. This can raise your sexual energy and is a great place to begin for couples who have been sexless for a long period of time. We can get so caught up in focusing on orgasm that we miss the beautiful sensual moments in between. Tantra focuses on reverence, in the moment. It brings back the sacredness of sex, which many of us have lost. Instead of using your partner for personal gratification, the focus is on giving to the other, and then receiving.

Prior to studying and experiencing Tantra healing a piece was missing for me. My energy would rise without culminating in orgasm. It was as though my orgasms were choked off. Healing the sexual trauma took courage. However, I knew if I was going to be totally orgasmic and stand in my personal power completely, it was part of my healing journey. When women begin to function in their power, with regular orgasms, they are much more centered, powerful, and complete. We become the Goddess.

This is one of the life-changing events I assist non-orgasmic women with. I know first-hand the frustration that many women endure by not being able to have an orgasm during sex. Being non-orgasmic affects our brains, electrical circuitry and enlightenment. When our energy rises in orgasm, we can feel the surge up our spinal column into the frontal lobe of the brain. This experience is a brush with God. It is the closest we can be, in human form, to The Divine.

O-No!

Living without orgasm shrinks a woman's feminine power. The physical and emotional frustration of being left out in the cold is one I don't like to see anyone live with. Living in an orgasmless world is not living fully. Unless many women self-stimulate, they just don't get there. Believe me, you don't want to have to go into the bathroom after your husband or boyfriend is fast asleep to masturbate. Or worse still, lay crying yourself to sleep with frustration feeling alone and neglected. Guys, women will have sex with you more often if they reach orgasm regularly. Men complain that women don't want sex. Would you, if you didn't come?

Women need to compassionately teach their men how they want to be made love to. We can't expect men to know. Women often allow events to happen without steering or making suggestions. If we are considerate, kind and compassionate with our men, they are more apt to give us what we want. For men, it is your job to make sure, that your partner has an orgasm. (I am hearing male readers ask, "Oh is it my job to get her to come?" Yes it is fellas, every time. Not just once in a blue moon. Let me ask you this question: do you expect your partner to bring you to orgasm? Of course you do. I rest my case.)

My husband's bruised ego along with his resultant pouting and rage (caused me to remain silent about my lack of orgasmic bliss. I have listened to many women since that time with similar issues. Women are not having orgasms and are remaining silent about it. During the hundreds of interviews I conducted, many women have said to me, that women have created this false reality that all men are studs by faking orgasm. We have to take responsibility for being where we are.

Taking responsibility for what we have created is just the beginning. This issue is global, not regional. I have heard women complain from all over the world. Men are coming, but many women never do. Women get what they get, which is usually a quick on-and-off event in which most women are rarely pleasured to orgasm.

Our cultural landscape has made sex about the

male's priorities in any relationship. Women have been the pleasure palace of men for eons. Many men, after having an experience with one woman, are off to the next hottest conquest. Although, not considered the norm, women can also jump from bed to bed.

Woman's vaginas, for men, are the donut hole on the concession stand of life that they derive pleasure from.

I recently had a discussion with a woman named Maria at the gym. Maria explained that in thirty-five years of marriage she thinks she might have had one orgasm. ONE ORGASM IN 35 YEARS! Because she only experienced it once she had nothing else to compare it to. So she wasn't completely sure that she had that one orgasm. How sad. Maria finally got up the nerve to tell her husband she wasn't having orgasms. When she did, he held a pillow over her face and punched her, then he screamed at her, "you're a cold potato!" Clearly the issue was that she was a potato, and a rather cold one at that. This is exactly the reason that women have remained silent.

Men, if a woman tells you she didn't come, is it her problem or yours? Think of it this way: who do you go to when your dick is hard? Do you wake up in the morning like a heat-seeking missile, looking for a hole to land in? Do you make your saluting soldier her problem? You know you do. So her orgasm is your issue. Men have to become the master of the female vagina. Ask her lots of questions (your partner, not her vagina). Through the Hunt and Peck System, HPS, you will learn what pleases her and do it EVERY TIME, not just on her birthday!

Most men would probably be gnawing their own leg

off after thirty years without orgasm. Frankly, it is surprising to me how many of us have not received at least one orgasm each time our men want to have sex with us. Getting off is expected by most men. It should also be a given for women. Many women stop having sex because it's not worth it to them. They would rather self pleasure or shut down their sexuality completely, subjugating their womanhood to the male ego. Women stop missing sex. Many post-menopausal women need to have their pump primed again because their hormone levels are so low. Having regular sex through menopause and beyond is possible and will keep hormone levels higher.

Gentlemen Start Your Engines!

Orgasm for Life was written to help change the way men and women think about sex. When women are able to experience orgasms, they step into their power, becoming their Goddess selves. Without expressing all that they are as a woman, their life experience is diminished. I would like men to put themselves in the shoes or lingerie of their partner. Could you imagine having sex once, a week, twice a week or more and only getting the RPMs up to about 2,500. What if your engine never reached full power? What if you only revved up to 1,500 RPMs? How would you feel then? That is what over 40% of the women worldwide feel like all the time. They may get wet, they may get aroused, but they never make it to Disney Land! Just because a woman is wet, does not mean she is ready to go.

Speaking of partners, strangely lesbians are not any

better at pleasuring their partners than men are. If women don't know how to please another woman, how do we heterosexual women expect a man to be able to please us? We have to learn about our own bodies and what we really like. We have to experiment with different types of touch. We need to try new things. We need to touch ourselves to find out what feels good. Doing the same thing over and over will not give you different results. That is just crazy thinking.

Are you wondering how to spice up a hum-drum sex life? Do you ever consider using fantasies or role playing? Do you wonder if that constitutes cheating? Could you even bring up the subject? Leaving this book in the bathroom, with pages highlighted, or corners dog-eared may be enough to ignite some passion for you and your partner. How about reading the "how to" sections together? I seriously considered laminating the pages to make them more user-friendly. A sponge-and-go book, if you will! Perhaps I'll offer a water-proof version for my second edition.

The purpose of this book is to assist you to improve your communication and increase passion, compassion, tenderness, understanding and kindness. When there is greater understanding of each other's needs both will reach bliss and ecstasy with regularity. Through regular blissful sexual exchanges relationships open and flower. The love between partners becomes deeper and more meaningful. It is my desire to assist you to build intimacy through authenticity, and become a better lover in the process. Orgasm for Life bridges the gap of connectivity between the sexes. In so doing, each person gains the ability to understand while giving their partner what it is they want. When communication is improved outside the bedroom, we can be more open inside the bedroom. Then, each person can express themselves more completely with profound growth towards spiritual sexual union.

If men could understand that living in a non-orgasmic state is like shutting down half of your brain and a third of your body, can you imagine what life would be like if only half of your brain cells fired? What if you never had an orgasm, ever? You would then understand the mounting frustration and resentment that is present in more than 40% of the female population. It is a wonder that more crimes of passion are not performed by unfulfilled women. And men talk about your blue balls!

Everyone has different motivations for sex. Some people want to show their partner how much they are loved. Others have sex to feel healthy, vigorous, or alive. Many men have sex to relieve pressure. While others are having sex simply to get off. Whatever your motivation, are you ready to make amazing sex a priority in your relationship?

Sex Is The Glue

Sex is the glue that can hold a relationship together. Do you want to be a better lover while keeping your woman interested in you? Want to increase the sizzle to create more happiness, pleasure and love in all areas of your life? Are you a woman who has had sexual trauma, but never had an orgasm? Are you wondering how to stimulate yourself to a really big "O?" Men, do you wonder how to romance your woman? Are you wondering how to get her over the orgasm hump so that she can have multiples, or maybe just one? Want to know all his erogenous zones to drive him wild? Most women are probably thinking that there is only one, his penis! There are actually many more than just his Johnson! Or are you wondering how to give him the best blow job ever? Do you want to learn how to give your woman the best oral sex and love-making experience ever? Do you have questions about your G-spot, the A-spot, or how to stimulate it or where to find it? Does it really squirt? Are you wondering how to put back the "Ooooh" back in oral? Join me in a state of bliss. Come along with me!

Chapter Two
Round Peg in a Square Hole

*The way we communicate with others and with ourselves
ultimately determines the quality of our lives.*
—Anthony Robbins

MEN AND WOMEN HAVE had the natural desire
to join together for physical pleasure since the dawn of
creation. The exquisite male and female bodies were
created to fit beautifully together in sacred union. A
man's erect penis was created to fit perfectly into the
soft round opening of the woman's vagina. Both men
and women secreted mucous-like substances that were
slippery to the touch. This substance acted as a lubricant
for their bodies to fit together seamlessly, like oil
lubricates pistons of an engine. These exquisite puzzle
pieces were meant to couple like bacon and eggs or
beans and wienies. We were created for pleasure, not

just to maintain our species. If sexual union was not meant to keep a couple closely connected, we would only have physical desires when the female form was ripe for conception. Sexual desire is a perfectly natural, healthy, harmonious experience. We were created to come together for unification in sexual expression by experiencing bliss without remorse, guilt or shame. As a matter of fact, if we are not (having regular sex) we're not fully expressing ourselves in our natural or true state. Sexual desire is as natural a human need as is our thirst for water.

Men and woman were created differently, yet fit together so perfectly. Men need sex for intimacy. Women need intimacy to have sex. Women's need for intimacy prior to sex can be a problem for men who have had their needs stifled. Often what occurs is what I call a Mexican standoff. Historically a Mexican standoff was a confrontation with three opponents. Each one armed with a gun. The first to shoot is at an obvious disadvantage. If he shoots first, the second person will shoot him. So all three stand there waiting to see who will make the first move. No one wants to go first in relationship standoffs. No one wins in this scenario. Women refuse to be intimate until their man becomes intimate (opening up). Many men often refuse to be intimate until he gets off, preferring to orgasm quickly without concern for his female partner. Only the man wins in this scenario while the woman remains generally unfulfilled and angry, as usual. At least this gives us something concrete to complain to our friends about. Women often bond with one another by complaining about their bed partners.

Different Operating Systems

Our inability to communicate seamlessly is what keeps us apart. Our operating systems differ. The operating system of a man is very simple. Give him good food, regular sex, then most men are happy. Whereas women are much more complex. Women require romance, conversation, to be acknowledged, appreciated, feel loved, look beautiful, wined and dined, given gifts, hair done, nails polished, clean sheets, laundry folded, kids in bed, dog walked, dishwasher emptied, lunches made and enough time to sleep. Yes, we have a very long list of tasks we need to accomplish in a given day. When they are undone, they play heavily on our minds and plague us when we attempt to have the slightest bit of fun. Helping us accomplish some of our chores will free us up to ride that wild bronco of yours more often.

Direct Connect

Men communicate directly, saying what they mean, for the most part. Women, on the other hand, rarely say what they are thinking. Their words only hint at their meaning. Rarely do women ask men directly for what they want, especially in the bedroom. This makes them, from the male's perspective, difficult to understand and communicate with. There is an unconscious need to keep men guessing. Historically, women were more sensuous and sexy when they were mysterious. Many women have no idea what they want. We think we do.

Often when we get exactly what we wanted, we are plagued with irrational disappointment that we didn't choose differently, which makes it almost impossible for a man to please us. As Whitney Cummings, the comedian says, "You can't Fuck with that kind of crazy!"

Knowledge is power. This book will give you the power to pleasure, communicate, and grow. You will be the King in your bedroom. Women will learn to receive while being the Queen of their domain. They will understand themselves as well as their own physiology, so that they know what feels good for them. When women understand what feels good for themselves, they can better guide their partner.

Drill Sergeant in the Bedroom

We all have emotions from egos. Most of us are very sensitive when it comes to criticism in the bedroom. We can feel so vulnerable when we are totally naked in front of another person. Asking for what we want needs to be done with care along with loving support, rather than criticism. The good news is: there is a way. Instead of yelling at your partner, "Drop down and give me twenty!" Giving a complement for what your partner did well always needs to proceed, "Can you use more tongue, okay baby that's the spot!" Staying quiet within the confines of a marriage or partnership about your needs to keep your partner's ego protected creates anger, resentment, usually resulting in mediocre sex. Most men know exactly what they like. They can describe what they enjoy in bed in exacting detail. When you can do the same for your partner, you will be hopping onto the pleasure pony. Are you ready for really great sex? When you have electrically charged orgasms consistently you will feel empowered, more secure, confident, and refreshed because you will tap into your inner power.

Rejecting Sex and Love

The bottom line is if he or she isn't getting it at home, you are pushing them out the door to get some with someone else. You can hide your head in the sand, but rejecting your partner's sexual advances is passive aggressive and abusive. Some would even call it torture. What is loving about rejection? I've got nothing.

In relationships where one partner is abusing, hurting, harming or causing physical or emotional pain, get out as soon as you can. No one should be hurting or harming you. Sex is not required in these relationships. It is very difficult to relax and let go when you don't know when your partner will harm you.

Rejected and Neglected

When your partner turns you down for sex repeatedly, you may feel hurt, rejected, or unattractive. You may wonder what you have done to be cut off from physical contact and affection. You might even know what happened. When sex stops happening with regularity because one person doesn't want to, it can make you feel sad, lonely and cut-off within the relationship. Many feel vindicated enough to step outside of the marriage and have an affair. Without frequent love-making the rejected person may feel resentful, angry, or even spiteful.

Although this couple may remain together, pain and suffering can result. One or both of you may feel depressed. You might gain weight or begin drinking, masturbating, or fantasizing about co-workers or other forms of behavior. All these things can destroy a relationship. To be honest, I don't understand why one party would turn down a good Rogering. Ask your partner why? It might not be about you, but rather about them. It could be their job, pressure, depression. If you don't ask questions about what is wrong, you are missing the opportunity for intimacy, and repair. What if your partner is not feeling loved, attractive, or good enough? Asking questions can shift your relationship. It shows caring and compassion. What could I do, say, or offer to you that you would know that you are completely loved?

Rejection can have a huge impact on the jilted person's sense of self. In extreme cases, it could be that one party is just waiting for their partner to die to be free. This becomes a robotic existence of pain and suffering, void of any spiritual significance without love or caring. You are not living fully. In fact, a part of you is dying. You are just going through the motions of life, sinking further and further into depression and darkness.

I experienced the deep rejection and betrayal of an affair personally. When I recognized my last husband was having an affair I felt unattractive and depressed, and I wondered what was wrong with me. I could not understand why he had an affair when I never turned him down for sex. He returned from a solo ski trip and wouldn't even hug me. He turned me down for sex, but masturbated in the shower. His issue was deeper than I ever dreamed. He had been molested as a child, by an uncle. He was wrestling with inner demons in an attempt to make sense of what was going on internally. It had nothing to do with me. It was all about him. He was struggling with his own masculinity.

When I got passed my own denial of the issues, it was obvious. Had I been paying close attention from the beginning, I would have seen what my daughter did. He never kissed me passionately. Instead his kisses were smacks, rather than kisses. He preferred sex from behind, or oral sex performed on him, never opening his eyes to look at me. I was the wrong sex!

Rejection can happen for many reasons. Asking probing questions without judgment can help you both uncover the reasons for the issues. It could be that there is a mis-communication. Sometimes we become very upset with our partner over the smallest of things. Letting your mate know that you are concerned and want to work things out, can be all that needs to happen. Sometimes, all we need from our partner is to know that we are loved, accepted and cared for.

Till Death or the Money is Gone

To illustrate the polarities of sex in two different ways, I have included two real life stories.

Susan and Simon were happily married for nearly 20 years. Their relationship had weathered many ups and downs, as most do. Simon was a successful attorney who founded his own law firm, just prior to the down-turn in the economy. They lived in a huge beautiful home in an affluent community. His business diminished greatly causing them to have to sell their home and move into a much smaller home in a very different socio-economic area. Susan's friends changed when their status altered. It caused her great distress. Her own sense of worth diminished when they left their beautiful home. She unconsciously blamed her husband for their plight. Simon kept his sense of humor, for the most part, while he worked long hours, helped around the house when he could. On weekends he helped Susan entertain. They created fun, themed, dinner parties. All Simon wanted from Susan was regular sex. Susan felt that Simon was not connected to his heart and just wanted the physical aspect of sex. She was determined to not have sex with her husband unless he changed. Simon was shut down emotionally because of the rejection. He felt neglected and unloved by having his repeated advances denied. Simon became increasingly irritable, resentful and sniped at his wife. Susan took his sniping as a personal assault and dug her heels in deeper. She continued to refuse Simon sex. (A stand-off occurred with neither party wanting to budge.) Both were left frustrated and angry. The continued sparring took a serious toll on their marriage, impacting their happiness and that of their children.

George was a multi-millionaire stock-broker, traveling the world. George entrusted his home and money to his brother while he was away. His brother embezzled his money to the point that George and Claire lost their mansion and all that they owned. Destitute and broke they had to live in their car with their two children. Claire stuck by her husband, supporting him and loving him through these changes.

She wanted to help her husband and continued to have as much sex with her husband as he wanted to help him through the challenging days and nights. Regular sex helped George feel better about himself. George said later, that the only thing that got him through these difficult times was the support of his wife.

We can see that two couples had a very different outcome from similar circumstances. It is how we allow circumstances to color our intimacy and taint our relationships. Staying connected during challenging times through open-hearted communication and regular sex can turn difficulties into growth for both parties. For men, sex opens their hearts creating deep intimacy and more connection. When we refuse sex, they clam up and won't allow women in.

The bottom line is a sexless marriage is not a marriage at all. Eventually after years of mediocre sex, or no sex, one or both of the partners will either stray or divorce. Sex along with love and truthful communication, is the glue of our relationships. It allows men to open up and allow a women into his inner sanctum. Without sex, men shut down emotionally and generally will not allow women in. Women too, will find other ways to find satisfaction, or end the marriage. Being rejected by your partner can negatively impact your self esteem.

People will stay together in marriages where divorce is not an option. For others, when tension continues for too long one person may decide that they have had enough. A sexless marriage can help you decide to get out of a dead-end relationship that clearly isn't supporting you.

Sex, trust, and heart-felt communication are the keys

to deep intimacy. When both parties are involved and satisfied, it opens communication channels, helping to alleviate fears and discord. Sex helps to create and build trust in a monogamous relationship. When there is no discussion about an issue of sex, arguments can break-out, like brush fires. Before long, the small fires burn out of control. Small things become blown out of proportion. Sex helps to release tension within the relationship, breaking down the ego-barriers that we often create through our fears of intimacy, of being abandoned and or betrayed.

Married with Children

Commitment, honesty, and trust are what is required for deep intimacy. Sex is what lubricates a healthy relationship, keeping it young, alive, firing on all cylinders. Sex is a reward for many men, but often it is all too rare and fleeting. Most women in their 30's, with children, have sex once a week or less with their husbands. For men at this age, not having sex three times a week or more can feel like placing a four-course meal in front of a starving person and telling them they can't eat it. Lying next to your beautiful wife night after night, not being able to touch her is torture. Women can throw themselves into raising children, while having their tactile needs met during the day. When their husband comes home, sex is usually a very low priority. Sleep may be the only thing on a young mother's mind after a day of breast feeding, chasing, and raising children. Yet, to keep the marriage alive it needs to be a priority. Regular date-nights each week give a young couple the opportunity to get out without the children. Having grandparents watch the children at their home, can give new parents an opportunity to have sex without interruptions. A locking bedroom door is imperative for parents with small children. Keeping children out of the marital bed also helps to keep passion alive. Making love with an infant in your bed is not healthy for any of you.

Private time for a couple is important for keeping a relationship balanced, healthy, connected and growth oriented. At the same time spontaneity is necessary to keep the passion alive. When all your sexual encounters are planned, pressure to perform can cause issues and stress. Sex is supposed to be a fun, pleasurable experience, rather than feel like work. Having to become passionate on a clock or calendar certainly eliminates spontaneity.

Believe me, being a single mother is not glamorous. It can be one of the most challenging times in your life. Keeping your marriage alive and healthy is best for everyone. Children need two parents to be confident, effective, balanced adults. Making sex a priority means that you are making your husband a priority. He is needed as a parent and partner. Don't ignore him. For you men, just because your wife is a little more round than usual, make sure she knows you still are attracted to her. Women give a lot up to have babies. Men need to be understanding of their wife's needs as well. After giving birth, pregnancy can be the very last thing a woman wants. The fear of pregnancy can keep her from wanting to have sex. Use protection, to help dispel these natural fears. Be respectful of one another's feelings. Remember how much you loved each other before the pregnancy. That love is still present, under the diapers, laundry, and new obligations.

Surprising as it may seem, men and women often want the same basic things. Go to any Internet dating site to read the profiles. Men want a partner to share their experiences with, the same as women do. Each one of us wants to love and be loved. We all want to be accepted for who we are. Most of us want to have our physical needs taken care of. We want our sexual exchanges to be exciting, fulfilling, and beautiful. We want our partners to care for us and adore us, attracted to our physical bodies. Most want to have passionate sexual exchanges that include orgasms. We also want to be loved, appreciated, and respected for who we are.

Being Right, and Losing the Relationship War

Where we can get mis-directed is when we think of the opposite sex as the enemy. Relationships do not have to feel like war. Blaming our partners for how we feel is ego-based, codependent behavior. It is not productive while putting us in the position of victim. None of us are victims. (I have flogged that dead horse in my first book, *Odyssey Victim to Victory*.) This is my own story of recovery from childhood molestation. It holds keys to loving yourself and become a fully functional independent, sexual being.

No one wants to be made wrong. Our egos get in the way, with finger pointing. When we are told we are wrong, we can shut down emotionally. We cannot listen fully. We stop being able to hear what other person is saying without being reactive. The issue with wanting to be right causes us to be so focused on being right, that we miss the truth, the good stuff—the loving. We make our partner angry. We make our partner wrong. Our egos become activated and we run away from connection, closeness, and intimacy.

Instead of pointing fingers at the other person, it is more productive to look at why you feel the way you do? Usually our reaction to what the other person has said has nothing to do with why we are angry. We are often triggered by our partner, which is to say, we are reacting to an old wound or button placed within us by a family member, usually a parent, relative, teacher or close friend. Often the screaming is loudest when we pick at the scab of old wounds. It is our old wounds that need to be healed to be able to move on from the past, rather than being stuck in our stories. We can become so focused on what happened in the past that we feel our current partner is also doing the same thing to us. Our patterns resurface like an old broken record that repeats the same refrain until someone pushes us beyond where we have gone before. Which is why I so love the healing aspects of working with hypnotherapy and energy healing. I see my coaching clients move beyond their stuck-ness, with control and rigidity into fluidity and forward movement. Their fears fall away while ease and trust with happiness build. Using a hypnotherapy process to release the trigger mechanism, I have witnessed clients move beyond their fears, embracing the love and the beauty within.

Issues with challenges in life will always arise. Using words like "never," "always" and "should" create issues. Jonathan Robinson, author of *Communication Miracles for Couples: Easy and Effective Tools to Create More Love and Less Conflict,* uses a wonderful, easy way to help couples resolve conflict effortlessly. Robinson says we each have a self esteem bank account. The lower our self esteem is, the less we can take criticism or finger pointing. We need to feel acknowledged, appreciated as well as accepted by our partners.

I agree with this concept having come from a place of low self esteem as a child. When my husband criticized me for something I was doing, it sounded like my parents were speaking to me. I went back emotionally to my memory bank, to the place of not feeling acknowledged and accepted as a child. Our minds are so powerful. The tapes re-wind in a millisecond. Instantly we are like a little child, rather than a mature adult. This often happens with couples. It is not what is occurring in the moment that has them upset. It is the connecting of the dots from this moment to a point in time that was painful. When we argue, often it is two children who have been wounded that show up rather than the adults that we are. Two little wounded children cannot resolve anything. They tend to pick up their toys and run away. This is a trigger mechanism. Until the trigger is cleared, this process will continue. This is one of my areas of expertise. My own experience of being reactive with volatility in relationships has made me an expert on uncovering these triggers for my clients. De-sensitizing them to the point that the trigger is no longer present, within one session—no more trigger!

Robinson's recommendation is to acknowledge how the other person is feeling first. Most of us that have been through therapy know about this tactic. However, his process goes on to create better communication with your partner. Acknowledging how they feel is not the same as agreeing with them. Once you acknowledge how they feel, they can hear you better. They feel validated, knowing you truly care.

Accept the other person's version of reality. This does not mean you agree. For example, Jane tells her husband, "I see how you feel blamed by me. " I'm very sorry you felt that way." Next, Robinson suggests that you tell your partner something that you appreciate about them when you are not angry with them. "You are really important to me, and I love the way you work so hard to take care of our family." Giving your partner something that you appreciate about them, allows them to let their guard down to feel less defensive.

The first thing that Robinson says we need to do when things get heated is to acknowledge the other person's experience. For example, as David is cleaning up the kitchen after dinner, his wife, Judith suggests, "Why don't you use this scrub brush instead of the sponge." David reacts, "Why do you have to nag at me whenever I try to help you?" His wife, Judith might retort, "I am not nagging at you, you just wash dishes like a two-year old and you need some help." Her off-hand, seemingly innocuous response might create a huge argument. David might think to himself, "She can kiss my white ass! I'll never freaking help her prissy little butt ever again!" David's little inner boy is showing up, because he feels wounded. Lower levels of self esteem make us more reactive and argumentative. Accurate, intelligent communication is a delicate art. It is the key to keeping a relationship balanced and communications open. When we are highly reactive, it throws up ego-barriers destroying closeness, open-heartedness, love and joy. Our little inner child (ego) is quick to judge or attack which shuts us down. What I believe Robinson is trying to show with this example is; how our egos can distort our communication, love-making and sexual functions.

If Judith had used Robinson's formula for communication, she might have said, "I hear you saying that I treat you like you're a child when you are doing household tasks. I am sorry that you feel I am putting you down." After being acknowledged, then validated, Judith's husband may relax feeling heard and understood. Judith would then let David know how much she appreciates her husband for helping her out, while lifting some of the burden from her.

Robinson reminds us, you don't have to agree with the way your partner is feeling. Remember, each of you is having your own experience. Three people can watch the same scene in a movie, and then interpret a totally different experience. We all have filters which change the reality we experience. These filters are created by our egos. Acknowledgement, says Robinson, creates trust. I believe, that the trust issues that Robinson speaks of is one of the most important issues in sexual functionality. The more you validate your partner's experience the more you build trust.

As an example, of how experience effects judgment; I was traumatized sexually by men, as a young girl. As an adult I made men wrong, because of what men did to me when I was little. I was tainted by my childhood experience. This experience created a lens that all men were bad and only wanted sex from me. I confused sex with love mis-judging my male partners. Men would say things to me, which I would take out of context. This created mis-communication and served to put a damper on our sexual activities. The key to having good sex and gangbuster orgasms is to see things clearly, rather than through our filters or egos.

Acknowledging that your partner is really having the experience they are, even if you don't agree with them allows them to feel heard. It also enhances communication and understanding. Understanding is one of the biggest issues within our relationships. We sometimes think very differently. We often come from various backgrounds. Our issues and trigger mechanisms can be totally unrelated. Each of us is having our own individual experience of the same thing. It does not mean that your perception is wrong. Accurate perceptions however, bring each of us nearer to the truth, regardless of our individual perceptual bias.

Having conflict resolved immediately keeps the air clear. Replying, "I'm fine!" When we are not, keeps us tied up in illusion and separation. We make up stories in our heads based on our past, which have little bearing on reality. This process should be avoided if you want good sex and great orgasms. The fragility of the human psyche guarantees that conflict will occur as our egos clash between male and female in the sexual act. It is also the point at which we can have the deepest connection.

An Apology - The Shoo-in

If conflict is left unresolved, it could be a cold snowy day in Miami before you have sex again. Women can't fight with their partner during the day, then cartwheel into the splits in bed ready to open their legs at night. Disagreements need to be resolved before bed-time if you want to have good oral sex. Going to bed angry is never a good thing. Sometimes we can't help it. A genuine apology and acknowledgement of our partner's experience can smooth the waters, opening the door to intimacy. I know several men who never apologized in all the years they were married. These men were just plain stupid. A genuine apology will get you more sex than flowers will. I was married to one of these stupid men. When the fairer sex are the only ones apologizing, there will be more snow in Miami! There are many things to be remembered for, this is not one that should go down in the *Guinness Book of World Records*! It takes a really big person to apologize and a small one to hold a grudge. That apology will get you more loving than you ever thought possible. Just make sure you mean it.

Women are emotional creatures. We need romance, appreciation, acceptance and to feel loved. Women don't feel loved when dinner has been criticized or we have been berated. We won't have sex with our partners if they don't apologize for being an ass. We are different from men. Our mind has to be in the game, or we simply turn off. We can be really stubborn creatures at times. I have known women to hang onto anger for months. Forgiveness is better for you than the person you forgive. When you are able to let go of the past, you will be much more likely to become ecstatic in the bedroom.

Make-up Sex

Make-up sex and angry sex can be wonderful. The passion can feel great at the time. However, the issue with make-up sex is that you can program yourselves to get into fights, just to have make-up sex. Repeating a negative pattern is setting the relationship up for failure. You will find yourselves fighting frequently, which can become an addictive pattern. This is unhealthy for the relationship.

Men don't feel loved, appreciated, acknowledged, or accepted for all they do whenever we reject them. Sex helps men feel loved and accepted as well as appreciated. Don't underestimate the power of appreciation, whether it is a project completed, a delicious dinner, or the best oral sex you have ever had. Say thank you like you mean it! Appreciation shows your partner that you acknowledge what they have done for you. It shows that you are not taking them for granted. Appreciation could be a meaningful hug, thank you or a bouquet of flowers to show you care about what they have done for you. Complementing your partner for a specific kindness shows that you noticed and appreciate their thoughtfulness. Appreciation is one of the biggest issues in long-term relationships that can show how much you care, changing resentment into love. Telling your spouse how much you love them, with meaning is important and often forgotten as years go by. We become flippant, voicing the words mechanically. This is not the same as saying, "I love you" from your open heart, like you mean it.

Communicating Through Our Heart

How we communicate our desires to our partners can make or break a relationship. Through careful, compassionate communication, both partners create deeper intimacy. Feeling a deep sense of connection, while teaching each other sexual preferences, through your sexual expression creates a more connected relationship.

Connecting your heart with your genitals shifts pure sex to an expression of tenderness and love. Rather than mechanical sex focused on technique, a sense of presence with connection during your love-making, shifts your relationship from that of spouses, or partners, to lovers. This deeper connection can enhance your orgasm while lifting sex into new spiritual realms. To do this close your eyes and envision your sexual energy in your genitals, envision this energy moving upwards and into your heart. You may have to do this several times to get the hang of it. To assist you, have your partner touch your genitals and then move their hand up to your heart, tracing the energy path with their hand, holding it there for a few seconds till you feel it in your heart center. You can also move the energy from your genitals to your heart by placing your right hand on the center of your chest, your left hand on your genitals, slowing your breathing down, and envisioning the energy moving up to the middle of your chest.

Love-making is not an experience that just happens in the bedroom. You can make love throughout the day, via text, a hug, squeeze of your partner's hand, or even a kiss out of the blue on the back of their neck. To separate your connection of love-making from the rest of your life downplays your bond. Having deep fulfilling hugs, with meaningful touches throughout the day lets the other person know you care about them and appreciate them at other times, not just when you want sex.

Close Encounters of the Non-Sexual Kind

Touch that occurs apart from the bedroom shows your partner they mean a lot to you. You can say a great deal without speaking, through meaningful glances and passionate touch. We are all about the sexual experience. Here, however, I would be remiss if I did not express that non-sexual touching will win more brownie points than a smack across the ass, or a boob grab during the day. Those grab-and-go touches can cause annoyance or undermine your partner's self respect. Playfulness has its place and can be fun. Make sure you are being respectful, by understanding your partner's innate desires.

Orgasmic Bliss

Deepening intimacy through total transparency and honesty, with open accurate communication will bring you closer when it happens outside the bedroom. Without a deep connection on the spiritual plane, sex is merely banging body parts together. Sex becomes an empty physical exchange, of lower level recreation or sport, rather than one of a higher mind-body-spiritual connection. When you can put aside all differences, then come together with the purpose of mutual pleasure, free of ego, our worlds collide with blissful exchange unknown up until now. Then, the higher planes of sexual, spiritual love begin to come into view. This is the place of orgasmic bliss.

Chapter Three
Hunt and Peck

Respect is one of the greatest expressions of love.
—Miguel Angel Ruiz

Men - Exposed

CONSIDER THE MALE FORM for a moment. He is naturally hairy and his genitals hang outside of his body. When he is aroused, there is no hiding the bulge in front of his trousers. When relaxes, his scrotum is in constant motion. When he is hot, they drop so that their precious cargo, sperm, stays fertile. Too much heat in the kitchen could kill the sperm. When he is cold his scrotum takes the elevator to the top floor and hug his body. Just this simple up-down process has got to be annoying. If nothing else, the constant sensation I would think would be a sentence stopper. Having all that sexual paraphernalia outside of a man's body draws his attention to it because it moves around when he walks. When you think about it, having all those body parts in constant motion would make it impossible to think about much else. This is probably the underlying reason that men think about sex every 52 seconds.

Men's external sex organs are representative of their communication style, upfront and exposed. Men rarely hide what they think. Like their exposed body parts, when they are upset or angry, they let you know. When you ask a man what he thinks, he'll tell you straight.

Women - Hidden, Buried and Covered Up

Women on the other hand have their beautiful lady parts tucked inside. Our vaginas are protected by our labia, which don't flap or move in the breeze. They stay put. Our clitoris does not jiggle when we walk and our labia majora does not shrink with the slightests breeze. No one knows when we are aroused by a thought, movie, or book. Our slacks don't form a telltale tent over our erect clitoris. Our vaginas remain faithfully tucked away, out of sight and out of mind. They don't move around when we are cold, or hot and never give our arousal away. A woman's sexual parts are lady-like and well hidden. They sit and stay when told. Women could be walking around in a constant state of arousal and no one would know. Our emotions too are often hidden, cloaked in a fake smile, or a quiet, "I'm fine!" When asked we rarely tell you exactly how we feel. We keep a lot of our feelings in the shadows, often in an attempt to keep peace. We are often difficult to read and even harder to please.

Women often think that men are insensitive. That is simply not true. They have sensitivity; they just aren't very sensitive to a woman's needs. They don't understand women, which is not surprising. They may not be able to communicate the way women want them to, but some can be just as sensitive emotionally as women, if not more. Their needs are simple. Most men are happy if you give him sex when he wants it, fill his belly when he is hungry and treat him with the respect he deserves. When happy he will treat his woman like a queen. Men enjoy sex when stressed. Most can go from zero to sixty seemingly at the speed of light. Within two to ten minutes he can be happily falling asleep on his pillow right afterward. Sex calms and relaxes men.

Women are far more complicated. We rarely tell our men what it is we need, and expect you to just intuitively know. For those men not equipped with psychic abilities, you are probably left in the dark when we get upset for seemingly no reason at all, then go storming off telling you "we're fine!" Most women feel that their men don't understand them. However, it is a rare woman that can communicate what it is she really wants. When it comes to sex, only the bravest have the courage to tell you what does and doesn't feel good to us in the bedroom. We might be a chatty Cathy in the kitchen, but "mmmm" is the word in the bedroom.

Moving Mountains and Women - One and the Same

It may seem you have to move a mountain to please

a woman. Most women need to have certain criteria to be met before having sex. They need to feel secure, safe and have trust in their man. Women need romance, soft candlelight, and music at the very least. Women need to be appreciated and thrive on romantic dinners, gifts, or flowers and to be told that they are beautiful. They need to be stress free, or they can't let go. Their man could be pounding them like there is no tomorrow, while she is focused on all the laundry that needs to be folded, the school lunches that need to be made or counting ceiling tile. She might even mentally write her grocery list while you are yelling, "Yes! Yes! Yes!" Women stress about what has not been completed and will think about those things during sex. Women need to be told that they taste good and smell even better. Most of us are very sensitive about vaginal odor and won't feel comfortable having oral sex if there is any doubt. Women need to have their head in the game or their sexual experience will not give them the pleasure or stimulation to get them all the way to orgasm.

Women want their partners to be clean and fresh from a shower. Expecting a woman to give you a blowjob when your balls smell like musty mushrooms or sweat won't win you mind-blowing sex. Seriously! Would you go down on yourself if you smelled that bad? Everything you eat goes through your body. Even down to your balls. Garlic, onions, and other strong smelling foods make your balls smell like yesterday's leftovers. Note to self, "Must shower before sex!" (This is true for both men and women.)

We love men for how easily they can be turned on. We love that we can get you to come with such ease, most of the time. The joke that men only have enough blood supply to run one brain at a time, is true. When men get turned on, they easily turn off all thoughts of work, the car needing an oil change or what time they have to be up for work the next day. Most men are very easy to please. We love that about you. We often wish we could be more like you.

What Turns a Man On?

In a nutshell—everything. Just walk in front of a man naked and your job is done! Men want you to touch their penises, end of story. Men can get a hard-on by being kissed. Oxytocin is released in a man's body, which arouses him through kissing. If you haven't touched his penis yet, now would be a good time.

Men and women also have vast neurological differences. Most men spend the majority of their day wondering when we are going to touch their penises. As soon as we do, they wonder when we will touch it again. Women's brains turn to sex only once in twenty-four hours versus most men's every 52 seconds according to Louann Brizandine, author of *The Female Brain*. It gives one pause to wonder how men actually accomplish anything during the day.

Men's bodies are bathed in testosterone, which is a key component causing him to think of sex so frequently. Women are also governed by hormones that affect her values, desires, what's important to her, and even whom she loves. Ms. Brizandine's findings also explained why women value communication as one of the key components of a relationship. Women speak 250 words per minute, while men use only 125. In an entire day, a woman uses 20,000 words, while a man only uses 7,000. Women also know intuitively what others are feeling, while men are busy thinking when someone is going to touch their penis next? Sometimes men are thinking of other things, but every 52 seconds he is thinking of when he'll be in the sack next having his penis worshipped.

When women communicate with other women, they prefer to face each other making eye contact. They listen intently to what the other has to say, using affirming sounds like uh-huh, umm, okay, which let the other know they are listening. They become emotionally involved in the other's story and may even cry together. A sense of closeness develops through sharing each other's lives. This type of communication rarely occurs in marriages. It is learned but not innate.

Men's communication style is a derivative of the hunter-gatherer days where they walked side-by-side, spread out across an open field. They worked together to track down and hunt prey. Today, men prefer to sit at angles to one another or side by side, without making intense eye contact. Conversation with men is action driven. They expect to resolve something by talking about it. They glance at one another on occasion, sitting quietly, rather than making sounds as women do. They rarely share deep personal situations preferring to engage in activities, like chopping wood, or riding bikes together rather than to sit and talk.

I recently visited a neighbor named, Greg, whose wife left him and his two small children for another man. We talked for hours about his situation along with how he was feeling about her betrayal. His roommate and he had never discussed her leaving. I found it so strange that these two men did not talk about something that was clearly such a profound emotional issue for him. He had no way prior to my arrival of bouncing his feelings off another. He was apologetic about the way he opened up to me. He commented he did not normally share such private details with anyone. It is not unusual for people to open up in my presence, pouring out their hearts and tears to me without me doing anything.

Sociologist Catherine Kohler Riessman reports in her new book *Divorce Talk,* that most of the women she interviewed with only a few of the men, site communication issues as the reason for their divorce. With divorce statistics being over 50% of all marriages, communication between men and women is the greatest issue facing us today. Most wives want their partners to be partners in conversation above all else, while their husbands do not expect the same of their wives. Sex is non-verbal communication. When sex is good, verbal communication is also.

Without good communication, sex and love are meaningless. When sex goes away, there is no way to dissipate the tension between a couple. Attitude, reactivity, and negativity contribute towards poor communication.

Sex is the unspoken communication between a couple. When two people are in synch, sex becomes an art form of fluid movement. It creates mutual pleasure. There is an unspoken understanding between two people that comes from the ability to communicate their desires or wishes verbally and nonverbally. The spoken word assists the non-verbal communication to be clearer.

We have seen the cartoon of the aging husband, cup

of coffee in one hand, with his nose in the morning paper. Pan to his wife looking angrily at the back of the newspaper, wanting to talk. Men typically do not express themselves the way women do.

Deranged and Confused

Women love to bounce ideas and problems off their partners. We work through our emotions by talking about situations. Usually we just want to vent. Men, on the other hand, often feel the need to fix the issue, then point out the other side of the problem. When women don't feel heard, they feel upset when men come up with a directive of how to correct the problem. Having someone else solve our problem for us can leave women feeling angry. What women want is a sounding board. Women don't want their problem resolved, they just want to be heard and understood. Women feel angry when their conversation does not net the result they were looking for. Sometimes, it is just a matter of support. Perhaps just understanding is what is really needed, rather than a solution. Women need to feel validated while being heard when communicating with their male counterparts or partners. Women typically aren't looking for resolution. Of course, it is not surprising that this can lead to confusion for men.

When men have a problem they tend to solve it themselves by running different scenarios through their mental software. Men tend to be more solution oriented. Most men talk about issues that need a solution.

Linguistics expert Deborah Tannen explains that men can appear dismissive and unsupportive to women during conversations because they have a tendency to shake off problems as being no big deal. Women become emotionally involved, often making problems bigger than men do. When men comment about our ability to make mountains out of molehills, it is like throwing gas on a fire. Women are more often caught up in the drama of other's than men, which creates further confusion. Why we would want to take other's problems on, leaves most men shaking their heads. It is just another way that we differ in our communication styles.

Men give women the impression they are not listening because they tend to look the other way, rather than make eye contact. Males often jump around from subject to subject. Women misinterpret this as not listening. Men may close their eyes or cover their face while a woman is speaking, giving their partners the impression that they are not listening. The differing perceptions can give us the wrong impression by misinterpreting or misreading the body language of our partners. Our perception of what is actually happening colors how we feel about the communication in our relationships. Our men may be listening intently, but their body language makes us think otherwise. Checking in with the other partner, while asking pointed questions will remedy any misunderstanding. Making assumptions and jumping to conclusions is what often gets women into trouble when communicating with our partners. Assuming sometimes connects dots that are simply not true. Being honest and open keeps communication clear, avoiding misunderstandings.

Even when communication is excellent outside of the bedroom, many women feel uncomfortable telling their partners what they want and need in the pleasure department. Childhood programming from parents, by society plays a large part in how women act in the bedroom.

Head Games - Good Girls Versus Bad Girls

Societal programming plays a large part for most women's bedroom etiquette. Many women in my generation lay quietly on their backs, rarely taking initiative or control over what happens when. Many women did not realize that pelvic thrusting, along with contracting their internal muscles would turn themselves on. Today's women however, are more sexually savvy and may already know these things.

In years past, many women shied away from giving oral sex because they felt it was disgusting or wrong. These same women may also feel insecure about having oral sex performed on them. In those days, Elvis and The Beatles were radical and wild. Teens today live in an Internet age, with well-advanced sexual exploits. Young people are exposed to sex everywhere. Television shows, commercials and billboards accentuate sexual promiscuity making it more acceptable by society. Girls are giving blowjobs at the back of school buses as early as elementary school. One example of how sexual norms have changed is that gay teens are coming out in middle school or earlier. With many reality television shows about teen mothers, younger girls are becoming pregnant, thinking it's cool. The morals from my generation have changed being replaced by the fast-paced on-demand society.

From early childhood these same little girls in my

generation were programmed to be "good little girls." Judgment still abounds. We see this every day. We look at others and judge them for what they wear, the color of their hair, and how they dress. My own daughter received glaring judgment from adult women because of the color of her hair, which happens to be purple at this writing. My daughter could feel "whore!" coming from women who had absolutely no idea who she was. After they heard her speak their viewpoint would soften.

If we judge others, we also judge ourselves. Being "good or bad" uses societal programming to pigeonhole others and ourselves. What this means to each individual can vary. Being a good girl could mean that you miss out on expanding the pleasure you receive because your underlying belief is that sex is dirty, bad, or ugly. For others, being "bad" can feel sexy and exhilarating. Being a mother AND a lover can feel incongruous or wrong. Some men have difficulty thinking of their wives as sexy, after giving birth to their children. Not because their body is misshapen, but rather that they have witnessed their babies coming out of the same place which used to be a pleasure playground, the vagina. Judgment can hinder our sexual expression and our joy.

Women are taught that bad girls talk dirty, writhe and moan with pleasure. Good girls, just don't. The point is that being "good" can also be construed as repressing your true inner nature. Holding on for dear life to all things lady-like can mean you don't let loose and let go. We hold in our stomachs, our butt cheeks when we walk and then expect to be able to have riotous orgasms. It just doesn't work that way. Women have been programmed for generations to please their men. But what about pleasing ourselves? What about receiving pleasure for you?

Our true inner nature involves fiery passion, moving, writhing as well as emitting sounds of pleasure. When we repress sound or movement, we reduce the amount of pleasure we allow ourselves to have. Emitting screams of ecstasy when receiving pleasure is a simple way to ratchet up the pleasure meter. It is unfortunate that such a natural, beautiful expression of love is being repressed. I have to admit that I never once heard my parents scream or moan with pleasure inside the bedroom. I was sure they never had sex! My parents were quite inhibited with their sexual expression. It was private. I did, however, hear yelling and screaming at other times— completely separate from love-making. Hence, it took a while and a lot of confidence before I was able to emit sounds and become uninhibited in private. What I came to recognize is that the times when I screamed or yelled without concern for anyone hearing me, I was able to achieve and receive more pleasure. Vocalizing (making sounds) increases pleasure for both parties. Just make sure your windows are closed or your neighbors might call the police. Or not, it could be one of your more memorable moments.

Trusticles

I have asked men why they cheat. Of course when I ask this question, I am assuming that they will tell me the truth. That is like going to a baseball game, buying a hot dog and expecting no wiener on the bun! Lying and cheating go hand-in-hand. The responses I have received are as different as the men I asked. Some say they cheat because they weren't getting any. Some cheat because they weren't getting enough. Some cheat because they just want to get back at their partner (the grudge fuck). Some men cheat because sex at home was boring, dull or meaningless. When an affair outside the marriage or relationship was offered, it was simply more exciting. In a long-term relationship sex often gets stale. This makes cheating more tempting. Some cheat because their wife or partner won't give them the type of sex they are longing for. This could be anal, oral, or kinky in nature. Some men cheat because their wife stopped swallowing after they got married, or never did. According to the men I interviewed, having someone swallow makes a man feel loved, accepted, and appreciated for who he is. Not swallowing is an act of disgust. It feels as though their lover does not accept them. (There are websites that teach women that this is okay and is no big deal.)

Engaging lovingly in oral sex sets the tone for a wonderful, blissful orgasmic experience. Oral sex out of obligation or fear does not get you to unbridled ecstasy or bliss.

Statistics paint a very clear picture. Over 50% of first marriages fail. Approximately 50% of women are unhappy with sex in their marriages. It is quite likely that this number is actually higher, because most women don't discuss their sex lives. Women site lack of communication as the biggest issue during their divorce. Typically, men don't look to a woman as a source of conversation. Men are not usually communicating with their women in the highest and best way that women want. When men are not open with their women verbally, women don't trust them. This lack of trust and open communication means that women are not wanting to have sex as frequently. Trust builds intimacy. Intimacy leads to better sex.

When a Man Loves a Woman

For you men, it is clear what you need to do more of. Be attentive. Listen. Be a sounding board. When you listen make affirmative noises, letting your partner know that you hear them. Only offer suggestions if you are asked. Don't be the devil's advocate unless she asks you to. In short, be more like a woman in your listening style. Certainly, we want a BFF, (best friend for life), a compadre as well as a lover.

Clear communication helps women feel heard. When women feel that they are heard and understood, they are more apt to trust their men. Same sex female partners don't have this communication issue. They already know how their partner communicates. Good communication helps establish trust. Women want to know their partner is there for them. They want to know they will back them up, support them, and understand them. If you listen to a woman outside the bedroom, she will be more apt to tell you clearly what she wants, because you won't be criticizing what she says. I have been very clear about certain things in bed with a man. For example, "Don't use so much lube—too much lube means not enough friction. I need to feel something and a lake of lube means I don't feel anything." Glop, glop, glop... a lake of lube anyway... "&*#%! Are you freaking kidding me?" I take the time to explain what I want, yet this man, clearly thought he knew better than I did what I needed! Not listening is one of women's biggest complaints about men.

Do you have any idea how frustrating it is to clearly ask your partner what you want then be totally ignored by them? Men like that rarely get a second chance. If someone tells you what they want, thinking you know better than they do is irrational and arrogant. Like George Carlin said, "Men are stupid and women are crazy!" Men don't listen and women keep hoping that their men will change—hence the crazy moniker.

Complex or Crazy?

Women may be more emotionally complex than men. However, what they really want is very simple. Women are looking for their partners to show up, be present, clean, listen, be supportive, and help out around the house. It may seem like a long list, but it will get you more of what you want. Men who help with traditionally "masculine" household chores tend to get more sex than men who do the laundry, dishes and household cleaning, according to a study by the American Sociological Association in 2013. It seems to be socially acceptable for women to perform more masculine chores, like taking out the trash or cutting the grass. However, in those marriages where men split "traditionally female" household chores, their sex lives declined in frequency. Frequency in sex is determined by gender scripts. The conclusion of this study is that men need to be helpful, but if they are doing the dishes to get more sex, forget it! You would be better off buying her some flowers, or taking her out to dinner to show your appreciation for all that she does.

Women and men don't like being told about our short-comings. We know we aren't perfect, but hearing what our issues are from our partners can feel like a slap in the face.

We have to able to take suggestions from our partners no matter what their sex is. To be able to grow together, we have to be adaptable to change. Change is inevitable, suffering is optional. We aren't perfect. We need to get over ourselves to move on. Letting go of anger and resentment is a must for healing issues within a relationship. Forgiveness and letting go is allowing forward movement. If we hold onto our anger of past issues, we are blocking love. We are saying "No!" instead of "YES."

Open Mouth Insert... Foot?

Men want their partners to have sex with them, give them head when they want it, take care of them but not talk so much. One of the biggest complaints I have heard from the men I interviewed is that women nag, complain, or talk about subjects that are meaningless far too often.

In women's defense, we nag because our men (and children) put us on ignore. When we ask our men to do something for us, we often have to repeat the same request numerous times. Women usually like their requests fulfilled or at least acknowledged immediately. When there is no response, we assume that you have not heard us. Being ignored can be construed as passive aggressive, disrespectful, and irritating. Remember turn-about is fair play, we can always ignore you in bed!

The flip side of this equation is that women often continue talking well beyond most people's reasonable limits. Being ignored is simpler and less rude that being told to "shut the fuck up!" When we go on and on, it is simpler to ignore us when we natter incessantly.

Typical jokes men tell about women have to do with how much we talk and how disinterested in sex we are. These may give women a clearer understanding of a typical chauvinists' attitude towards women.

Q: What is loud and obnoxious?
A: A woman.

A quiet man is a thinking man. A quiet woman is usually mad.

I haven't spoken to my wife for 18 months—I don't like to interrupt her.

Q: How do you keep a woman from wanting sex?
A: Marry her.

Q: Why did God make Adam first? **A:** Because he didn't want advice on how to.

Teenage Sex

Having teenagers decades apart has given me a good perspective of the phenomenon of the post Clinton administration. Teenage boys expect sex immediately. If girls don't have sex with them, they move on, because they can. Someone else will gladly spread their legs or give them head. Girls and boys are under the mis-impression that Fellatio and Cunninglingus is not sex. I've got news for everyone! If it involves a vagina or a penis, it's sex. Bill Clinton did not do anyone, including himself, any favors by lying over his misconduct in the White House. What he did do, however, is prove that you can't trust a politician with a hard-on to do the right thing.

Women often use sex to control their partners. This is not a proud moment for us women, but it is a behavior that has gotten us onto thrones, beheaded, married, raped, shot, stabbed, or even killed. Not having sex with our husband, partner, or lover is one thing if we aren't well. If we have a medical issue or pain somewhere that makes sex too uncomfortable, it is understandable that you would not want to have sex. Our partners need to be respectful of those times that we don't feel physically or even emotionally able. However, when none of those issues are present and we say, "NO," we are usually doing it to control our partner.

Teenagers are rarely mature enough to understand how to use sex as a weapon. Older women, however, who are more experienced, are quite good at manipulating their partners with sex.

Looking at the reason behind why you don't want to have sex, will give you insight to your avoidance of intimacy, pleasure and connection with your partner. Ask yourself who are you tormenting, yourself, or your partner? Pleasure, raising your sexual energy and feeling your partner's naked body can be a lot more fun than reading your romance novel, or turning over and attempting to sleep. You know you will sleep better after a lovemaking session. Perhaps you just don't feel like giving. If that is the case, why not tell your partner. "I don't feel like giving to you right now." If you will allow him to give you a massage, your mood will improve; you will burn a few calories and have some fun in the process. Sometimes, we get stuck in a paradigm that needs to be shifted. We get in our heads and make up all kinds of stories that simply are not true. If you are still saying no, why are you? Women can slide into the bitch archetype very easily. Are you just being a bitch? If you are, there are consequences to bitchy behavior. Remember sex cements your relationship. Being a bitch creates distance, disconnection and opens the door for affairs. I remember many times saying no, then lying awake wondering why I did so afterwards. I recognized I was holding out for ego-centered reasons, rather than being connected to my heart. I often said no, to have control over my own body, rather than just having to give of myself. In a loving relationship there is give and take.

To get out of your bitchy mood and open up to the unlimited possibilities of pleasure, take the steps below to shift your perspective:

1. Put your right hand palm side towards the middle of your chest, this helps you connect to your heart and get out of your head.

2. Take a deep breath. Hold it for the count of four and release. Exhale completely. Repeat twice more, for a total of three deep breaths.

3. Keeping your hand on your heart chakra, remember the last time you had immense pleasure. Think about how good it felt. What was the most

pleasurable sensation you felt? Before you say no, remember how much more connected you felt to your partner after being together physically. Touch your partner's shoulder. Make eye contact with your partner. Tell them you are hesitant but want to shift the way you feel. Ask him to do whatever it was that made your heart skip a beat first, before he enters you. It could be oral sex, a massage, deep kissing, or whatever your pleasure is.

Saying "NO" is a form of rejection and passive aggressive behavior. It is also abusive. Withholding love and affection is not loving at all. If you don't love yourself, perhaps you need to have some private coaching or do my Love Yourself Fearlessly course to fall in love with you. When you love yourself unconditionally you will have more than enough to give to your partner because you will be overflowing with love for you. You cannot give another what you don't have for yourself. Self-love is the cornerstone to happy balanced relationships. A lack of self-love makes you a victim, codependent and needy.

Sex Pistols and Other Weapons

Over the long, sordid history of sex on planet earth, both women and men have learned how to use sex as a weapon. From Cleopatra to Juliette, Marie Antoinette to Henry IIIX, sex has been used to manipulate. Sex within marriages is often transactional. We trade sexual favors for what we want. We may be married, or dating but this is still prostitution by definition. Women may be horrified by my clarifying of the truth. It is the oldest profession in the world for a reason. There is always someone who wants something and another who is more than willing to give it up to get what they want. Money may not exchange hands; using sex as a tool to get what you want is making sex a weapon.

The most balanced relationships do not manipulate or control. Both of these issues come into play when one or both parties are insecure or codependent. Fear is the reason people control others. The fear could be based on past experience or imagined behavior. A fear of losing control, or being cheated on can create issues, which divide and separate a couple permanently. The more confident and secure both parties are, the fewer fears that surface.

Sex is addictive, because the same pleasure centers in the brain that are stimulated by cocaine, gambling and money are stimulated by sex. Just as a mafia King in Vegas manipulates gamblers, a partner or spouse can manipulate us. Orgasms can be addictive because we want more of them. When people know that we want, our partners can use sex to control us. The promise of sex can be a powerful tool to get someone to do what we want. When the lower ego becomes involved, the addictive, destructive characteristics of sex can be turned into a formidable weapon. This is the opposite of what this book is about. Faking orgasms is a lower form of sexual behavior that manipulates or controls another.

Chapter Four
Faking It Till We Make It

The worst crime is faking it. —Kurt Cobain

Even THOUGH SOME PEOPLE do choose sex as a weapon, does not mean that you have to. Sex is so much better without it. Just imagine, your tongues entwine, your breathing becomes heavy. Eyes dilate with desire. You begin to feel the rising energy. Your heart rate increases, while your skin flushes with excitement. The sexual tension builds and its over! She vocalizes loudly spurring her partner on, so that he comes even harder. Then she sighs quietly with disappointment.

When a woman recognizes that she is not going to have an orgasm with him, she has several choices. To lay there soundlessly, or to assist him to have a stronger orgasm by faking one. When it is over there are several ways to go; encourage your partner to stimulate you manually to orgasm, masturbate in the bathroom, or attempt to sleep frustrated.

Faking it in the bedroom is not solving anything. Most women have faked it. You might think it is being kind to your partner, but at what cost? Faking orgasms is inauthentic. In the most intimate of moments you are lying to your partner. It leads them to believe that you have come. How do you think he or she will feel when they find out? Crushed, angry, betrayed, blaming, or possibly vindictive. All these things create barriers to intimacy.

Faking it is a lie. If you fake it during sex, you probably lie about other things within your relationship as well. Where else do you lie to your partner? This is a good place to be honest with yourself and make a list of all the areas that you lie to your partner and yourself. Faking it is avoidance of the issues at hand. I faked orgasms in my marriages for various reasons, as some women do. I have been married four times. After four marriages, I can guarantee you that if you continue to fake orgasms or anything else, these forms of deception will destroy your relationship. Faking it is a form of deception. You will have to deal with your untruthfulness at some point anyway. You might as well deal with it now. You are not doing yourself or your relationship any favors by hiding this truth. The fact that you are faking it means you are afraid to talk about a very deep and intimate issue. As you do one thing is how you to everything. If you fake orgasms, you lie about other issues as well.

Transparency is the way to go in open, honest relationships. Complete honesty, with nothing to hide, builds trust, and creates intimacy. Learning to talk about what you need and desire in the bedroom takes compassion and courage, so you can move beyond your fears of intimacy. In my third marriage, my husband Rich told me I had a fear of intimacy. I didn't believe him. I had to make him wrong. Truly looking into myself, confronting my fears of intimacy took me years to find out that he was right. Once I looked into myself and stopped faking it, I saw several important issues:

- I was afraid to ask for what I wanted, because when I did he became angry.
- I was embarrassed to admit that I had a sexual dysfunction, because it made me feel broken and insecure.
- I had tremendous fears of letting go and losing control. (As a child when I was molested, I began to feel pleasure. I blocked the pleasure because I felt guilty and ashamed, and made it wrong. The fear became frozen inside making a vaginal orgasm impossible.

Remember women whenever you fake it, intimacy is destroyed, distance is created, and your chances of getting or receiving a great orgasm are greatly diminished. Women have perpetuated the myth that our men are all great lovers by remaining mute rather than expressing our lack of orgasmic bliss.

Why Do Women FAKE IT?

According to a recent British study, 80% of women fake orgasm. Of the 71 women in the study, they reported being quiet when really receiving pleasure. This could be because the British are known for being stoic—you know, "stiff upper lip and all that rot!" Only 7% of women reported that they have orgasms through intercourse alone, without toys, oral sex, or other stimulus. This is not a mean-spirited act, however, it is still faking it. It is done to boost their partners self esteem. Women usually fake it because we don't want to bruise our partner's ego. Our sexual partners' ego can be a delicate thing. We fake it because if we don't, we may not get any sleep. We fake it because we don't want to hurt our partner's feelings. It is however, a form of manipulative behavior.

Schemers

A woman who fakes orgasm to get her man to divorce his first wife or gain money or some other nefarious desire or objective.

Screamers

A woman who fakes her orgasms loudly, screaming and carrying on to make her partner feel sexually powerful. She does this in an effort to manipulate him and his male ego to gain material things, such as money, a vehicle or drugs, paid for by him.

Star Trip Dreamers

A woman who is starry-eyed and co-dependent. This type of woman usually falls in love on the first date or first sexual encounter. She is the chameleon. She becomes anything that her partner wants, turning herself inside out, in an effort to win favor or please her man. She feels she has to do these things to be loved, because she hates herself. She feels unworthy, insecure and ashamed. This type of woman has usually been molested or abused in childhood. (This used to be me.)

These are just three ways that women can fake their orgasms to manipulate their partners. If you fall into these three categories, it is time to stop this form of faking it now. Instead talk about the issue and work together to create joy and bliss with your sexual partner to have the best orgasms of your life. Sexual healing may be needed to overcome sexual dysfunction. Admitting there is an issue is the first step to healing this problem. If you continue to fake it, the hope of changing behavior is negligible.

When we don't come, we can feel bad and often guilty because we feel like something is wrong with us. To be honest, I used to fake it. I did it because it took so long to get there. I felt it took an inordinately long time, so I was concerned that my partner was getting fatigued. This left me feeling insecure. I also felt very uncomfortable. I was more concerned with my partner's satisfaction than my own. I knew there was a better way. I had tried to talk about it, but my husband became very hurt, angry, and withdrawn. He felt threatened. If this happens to you, understand that you are not alone. Millions of women have had the same issues. Knowing the best way to approach this very sensitive subject helps. Always remember that faking it will ruin your sex life, destroy your relationships, and diminish your joy.

The typical woman needs twenty to forty-five minutes of foreplay (manual stimulation) to achieve an orgasm. The average man, on the other hand, lasts between ten and twenty minutes. (Gentlemen, please recognize that I am talking averages here. For some men it can be as little as two minutes, for others hours.) It can feel uncomfortable, or awkward for both parties creating pressure when an orgasm doesn't happen. As a result, many fake it to get sex over with. It makes you wonder why men and women were created with such different needs. The amount of time and attention most women need seems out of proportion to what men need. Some men get excited to the point of orgasm just by seeing their partner naked. As the comedian Whitney Cummings says, "How do you turn on a man? Take off his socks!" When it is so difficult for women to get there in the allotted time, It seems the kind thing to do—fake it. While faking it may win you brownie points in the short-term, in the long-term it can destroy the relationship and makes things worse.

For those women who need additional stimulation, there are many different solutions. Choosing a position that allows stimulation of the clitoris through vaginal sex helps. Placing a pillow under her hips, to tilt the pelvis upwards improves the positioning of the penis, so that it strokes the upper side of the vaginal wall. Sitting on top, straddling a man can be the only way a woman can come through vaginal sex. For a small percentage of women, this works some of the time. Coupled with digital clitoral stimulation this position can be very effective. Women need to get over their sheepishness about having to masturbate themselves to get there. The first time may take some courage. After that, knowing that you have the power to manually assist can empower you.

Many women don't feel comfortable masturbating privately, never mind in a partner's presence. From the many conversations I have had with men, they wonder why? Men are perfectly comfortable with women self-pleasuring. As time goes on women say "No!" as often as they do because they don't want further disappointment. My theory is that women are so disappointed with non-orgasmic sex that they feel it is better to turn it down, rather then get revved up only to be disappointed. If their partners knew how to stimulate them to orgasm, women would participate more often, and gladly.

Disenchanted Evening

Frustration from lack of fulfillment leads to anger and resentment. This is not anyone's fault. When you aren't satisfied or make a habit of faking it, you will eventually feel left out or even angry. When do you stop to face the elephant in the room; after 5 years, 10 years, or when you finally get a divorce? Women eventually become disenchanted with sex when the outcome consistently leaves them feeling flat, unsatisfied and frustrated. When women fake it, their men usually have no idea. After all, most men want to just have their own orgasm and roll over. They snuggle peacefully, thinking they have done their job well, and then fall asleep. Women, more often than men, are the ones left hanging, frustrated, unable to sleep after sex. Sex is supposed to be pleasurably fun, bringing you closer, not the other way around!

A block to intimacy is created by a lack of honesty. It is better to recognize that there is a disparity rather than to continue to fake orgasms. Talking about the subject without blame is important. Be compassionate with yourself and your partner. Telling your partner that you have not been having orgasms can be a shocker, if you have been doing so for a very long time. Breaking the ice is important. Don't blame your partner. Admitting that there is an issue, while you are willing to work through it is what is best for you both. The worst thing you can do is fake it till you make it. Letting go, or casting off your old issues can help bring you to joyful sex.

Casting Off

According to Unifem, one in three women around the world will be raped, beaten or coerced into sex, or otherwise abused at some point in their lives. Men too experience childhood molestation and rape, which create lasting issues of an emotional and sometimes physical nature. These statistics illustrate a sad story. Sexual dysfunction comes from sexual trauma. Getting help is important. Healing from trauma must occur for many men and women to be able to have a healthy sex life. Trust is one of the biggest issues that women face today. Without trust, it is next to impossible to let go and truly enjoy sex.

Men also may be dealing with the after effects of childhood molestation. The statistics state that one in six (although I feel that it is higher) men have experienced childhood molestation before the age of 18. Molestation often goes unreported for both boys and girls, because of shame or because a family member was involved.

Decades after sexual trauma occurs, I have found there is cellular memory in the sensitive vaginal walls that can make sex painful, with elusive orgasms for many women. With the fright, freeze or flight syndrome that occurs with sexual molestation, fear is frozen in the vagina, tops of the thighs and g-spot. This freezing is stuck energy, which can block orgasms from occurring. (This is discussed in Sexual Healing chapter.)

You are not alone if you have challenges completing the sex act without getting some help. Be honest. Intimacy rarely happens when you lie. Remember faking it destroys your sex life. Explain to your partner that there is an issue. Get help from a sex coach like me, a Tantrika, or therapist. (A Tantrika is a trained sexual healer that deals with sex, orgasms, and dysfunction.) There are plenty of Tantrikas who also help with sexual healing, dysfunction, along with all the other relationship issues they create.

9 MAGIC Steps to Reaching Orgasm

1. Get to know your own body and your partner well.

2. Relax, Breathe, keep bringing your mind back to the pleasure. Take your time. Keep focusing on the pleasure. Let go of other thoughts.

3. Eliminate distractions. Turn off the television and phone. Surrender to the feelings of pleasure.

4. Keep eye contact with your partner to stay connected, in the moment. Disassociative behavior will stop an orgasm.

5. Talk to one another. Tell each other how beautiful you are. When your partner talks to you and tells you how much they love you, how good you feel, taste and smell allows you to let go more easily.

6. Extend foreplay. A woman's body needs at least twenty minutes of touch, stimulation, massage, and arousal. Everyone is different. See my You tube video called the Female Orgasm)

www.YouTube.com/watch?v=9mWHcnkVjIc

7. MAKE SOUNDS. Vocalizing your pleasure will help you to let go and orgasm. Don't be concerned about making faces. You are beautiful!

8. Move your pelvis rhythmically. Pelvic thrusting can open up the energy channels causing sexual energy to move, which when allowed to build can create an orgasm. Squeeze your vaginal muscles (like kegel exercises) and butt cheeks in rhythmic movements to get your sexual energy moving up through the spinal column.

9. Open your mouth and breathe. The more relaxed your mouth is the more relaxed your body will be, as above so below. Relax your jaw. This will open you to receive pleasure and the unlimited possibility of orgasmic response.

Chapter Five
Anatomy of an Orgasm

There's a new medical crisis. doctors are reporting that many men are having allergic reactions to latex condoms. They say they cause severe swelling. So what's the problem? —Dustin Hoffman

EVERYONE WANTS TO HAVE orgasms in sex. An orgasm can precede the act of procreation after which children are born. Here are some interesting facts about orgasms that help us understand the nature of orgasm.

- Average duration of a male orgasm 3-5 seconds
- Average duration of a female orgasm 5-8 seconds
- Most number of orgasms in one hour 134 - woman
- Most recorded number of ejaculations in one hour 16 male

- Longest recorded orgasm 43 seconds
- A smile uses 16 muscles
- An orgasm uses 116 muscles
- Average heart rate during an orgasm 140 beats per minute.

Google describes an orgasm thusly: A climax of sexual excitement, characterized by feelings of pleasure centered in the genitals and (in men) experienced as an accompaniment to ejaculation.

A street definition of an orgasm: An incredible sensation lasting only a few seconds, generally costing way too much that can get you into way too much trouble.

If you have ever experienced an orgasm, you recognize that the definition barely scratches the surface of the enormity of an orgasm. It encompasses so much more than the sexual orgasm and ignores the fact that women can also ejaculate.

An orgasm can be an all-over body experience that is felt in every single cell. An orgasm can send an electric charge of energy up our spinal column into our frontal lobe that instantly changes our perspective on everything. No, an orgasm is not just in the sex organs.

Ray Masten is the author of The Love Guru pages, "How To Pleasure A Woman And Have Her Come Back Begging For More." According to Ray, women need to have their energy raised in preparation for lovemaking. He recommends that you begin in the morning if you want to make love in the evening. Women need attention, phone calls and to know that you are thinking about us. We need our hands held, eye contact and to know you care about us. We love flowers for no occasion. It shows forethought. You took time to stop and buy us something, rather than just showing up expecting sex.

What has been missing in our society is that there is no story about lovemaking passed down through the generations to teach our young people about sex. Father's rarely teach their sons about making love and pleasuring a woman, or even how to understand a woman. Most barely know how to themselves.

After over 80 years of research, scientists are still testing, probing and trying to understand what happens in the body-mind during orgasm. MRIs and laboratories are hardly the place to have an orgasm, but researchers at Rutgers University are doing their best to analyze what happens in the female brain when a woman stimulates herself to achieve the highest heights a human body can experience, inside an MRI.

Barry Komisaruk is a neuroscientist hoping to assist the climax challenged . His study has included two hundred participants who donated their most private moments to science. Each one stimulating themselves to orgasm in ten minutes. It makes your body rush with excitement just thinking about it. In fact, of the two hundred participants in this orgasmic study, one particularly gifted young woman of thirty was actually able to think herself off. Now that lady is one I want to meet! Can you imagine, "I think I'll get off, and then you come? An orgasm certainly encompasses more than just a penis, vulva, or vagina. An orgasm can contract over 116 muscles in the body and occur in 11 different parts of the female body.

An orgasm is the culmination of exquisite pleasure emanating from the perineum (root chakra between the vagina and anus or scrotum and anus) which surges up through the central channel or spinal column exploding in the 80 centers of the brain. If you slow down to notice the energy surge, follow it from the base of the spine, all the way up the spinal column along the back of the head into the frontal lobe of the brain. When you do you will experience an orgasm more fully by being present enough to feel the energy lighting up your brain. Your orgasm will take on yet another level of excitement.

An orgasm is the only event in a human's life that has the ability to light up all the centers of the brain like fireworks in a night sky. A flood of hormones rushes through the body, causing us to feel a deep sense of well-being—Oxytocin the hormone that is released during labor for women, and kissing in men. It also increases intimacy then deepens levels of trust in women for their partner. Endorphins also flood the body causing more powerful feelings of joy and bliss. Oxytocin has a darker side as well, which can cause feelings of jealousy.

An orgasm can happen with a flaccid penis. It can occur without ejaculation and still be a "soft-gasm." An orgasm can be experienced as an all-over the body sensation. An orgasm can happen by thinking it, without any physical contact whatsoever.

Orgasms differ from person to person. They can also be different each time they occur for the same person. Stimulus, environment, stress, music, lighting, thoughts, sounds trust, safety, the person you are with or the way you feel about them all influence the experience. An orgasm through self-stimulation can be just as pleasurable as one with a partner.

The Four Stages of Orgasm

Excitement Stage

As pleasure builds in the body sexual tension increases. It can give you the feeling of fullness. Heart and respiration increase, blood pressure rises. In women, the vagina begins to lubricate itself and the clitoris begins to swell. There may be a feeling of throbbing or a heartbeat inside the vagina, or penis as pleasure builds. The body experiences vasoconstriction (narrowing of the blood vessels.) The skin begins to flush with excitement while her breasts may swell as the nipples become erect. All this can happen in a matter of seconds, then last from minutes to hours (for both men and women).

During the excitement stage a man's penis becomes erect. The penis also can emit a lubricant also known as pre-ejaculate or pre-cum. Its purpose is to reduce the acidity in the waiting vagina that could potentially kill sperm. The amount of lubrication varies from man to man. Some men emit none.

Plateau Stage

The plateau stage is also known as the preparation stage. This is when the body prepares for orgasm. The body continues to experience a flush and may even tingle. Pupil dilation, sweating, and increased brain activity occur. Some people have the evidence of this flush in their faces. Remember being caught in your basement by your parents? Mine always knew when I had been kissing, because of my tell-tale flushed face. As excitement continues to increase, the labia minor (inner lips) begin to darken with the increased blood flow. Pulse and respiration have reached their peak. The deeper one breathes in this stage, the more ecstatic the body feels. Some women tend to hold their breath here, while they stop or stifle their orgasm and pleasure. Two minutes prior to orgasm the brain's reward centers become active. These are the same centers that are activated while drinking and eating.

For men, this stage can last from minutes up to an hour. It typically is the stage where the highest levels of excitement occur. Breathing and blood pressure continue to increase. The penis increases in size, especially around the glans or head of the penis. The testes swell and pre-ejaculatory fluid is often emitted.

Stage 3 Orgasm

The clitoris contracts under the clitoral hood, as the vagina tightens and lengthens. Vaginal along with anal spasms, occur rhythmically, causing wavelike contractions to move from the top of the uterus to the cervix. Muscle contractions also occur through out the entire body, including the neck, pelvis, arms, legs, and feet. The body becomes hypersensitive to touch. All 80 centers of the brain light up in orgasm, while the body is flooded with oxytocin, endorphins and dopamine. The brain totally checks out, this is not a good time to balance your check register! The release of oxytocin with sex makes women feel like they are in love. It causes us to be more accepting and trusting of others. If you don't want to be swimming in hormones, which make it difficult to see the truth early in a relationship, postpone having sex until you are sure about the person. If a woman has sex with someone just as a roll in the hay, she could get sidetracked in life with jealousy and feelings of love, but not really BE in love.

The difference between hormonally induced feelings of infatuation versus real love can be subtle. Infatuation can feel intense, as if you are carried away with passion, selfishness, and possibly obsession. These feelings surface when your relationship is purely sexual. Infatuation involves trusting when you have no reason to, often with a reckless abandon of wise choices. You may have an idealized vision of the person that may be totally inaccurate. You may feel insecure and attempt to impress the other person. Your focus is getting the other person to like you, rather than feeling secure, comfortable being yourself. You may act irrationally and uncharacteristically. If you experience conflict with this new person, you may be concerned that the relationship is over. Your focus may be on the way they look at you, the way they say your name or how they look when they smile. Your basis for analyzing your feelings is trivial, based on chemical or hormonal brain activity.

When you are experiencing love, you feel sure that the relationship will go the distance. You feel confident that conflict will not end the relationship. You have a desire to work through situations rather than abandon the relationship. You know each other well and can anticipate how they will react to a situation or conflict. You feel secure being yourself, and know that they will not bail with the slightest issue. You are willing to compromise and make situations work. Love makes your heart feel as though it will burst with feelings of intense affection. The outcome of real love versus infatuation is that love lasts, while infatuation is short-lived.

Having sex with someone new causes women to let their guard down, sometimes when we shouldn't. The release of oxytocin is often called The God Hormone, or cuddle hormone. It causes feelings in the body and brain that feel similar to love, but don't last like real love. We begin to trust when it might not be in our best interest to do so. Having sex too soon before you really know someone can cause you to make choices that can take years to recover from.

Oxytocin is the same hormone released in labor that makes women fall in love with their screaming babies. Nature had to create a way for us to love them. The release of oxytocin lowers a female's defenses, then causes us to trust the person we have sex with, unbeknownst to the conscious mind. One-night stands and sex with a stranger can be exciting, we just need to recognize the risks and keep our wits about us. Those hormones that make us love our screaming babies also do the same for screaming men. We often think we are "in love" when it is simply a rush of hormones in our brain and body.

Neuroscientist, Komisaruk believes that women have the capacity to experience a more intense and complex orgasm than a man. He, along with his researchers, have discovered that four different pairs of nerves—hypogastric, vagus, pudendal, and pelvic—carry information from the woman's genital area via the spinal cord to her brain.

The feeling of wanting to explode as the pleasure reaches its pinnacle. The pelvis becomes tense, toes, legs and feet may stretch, then release. As the orgasm occurs the tension releases, muscles contracted previously relax followed by a surge of pleasure causing dopamine with oxytocin to be released and flood the body. Dopamine stimulates the pleasure sensations as oxytocin does, which causes the uterus to contract. The entire body is flooded with the feeling of elation, then exquisite joy. Orgasm provides the body with a complete workout.

During orgasm, men reach the pinnacle of their breathing, muscle tension and heart rate. The pelvis contracts rhythmically. Ejaculation of semen occurs while the entire body contracts, then releases the built up sexual tension. There is a loss of the full erection. The penis immediately loses its erection and diminishes in size.

The Resolution Stage

The final stage of orgasm is called the resolution stage. During this time a sense of happiness or pleasure surges through the body. Contractions can continue in waves for several more seconds with diminishing intensity. There are many different types of orgasms that can be experienced; scientists have boiled them down to Type I and Type II. What has been scientifically proven is that similar levels of oxytocin and dopamine are released. There are similarities in heart rate and respiration rate as well. The blood that has been pooling in the body is released while the muscles relax deeply. The body goes from one extreme to another in a matter of seconds; deep relaxation with calm spreads through the entire body and mind. Both sexes have a general feeling of well being and sleepiness after an orgasm.

Without orgasm at the end of this surge of blood, pleasure and tension, usually the body will return to normal gradually. The sexual tension will release, over time then your body will return to normal. Often this stage can lead to frustration when orgasm does not occur. On rare occasions when the sexual tension builds, but remains high for exceedingly long periods of time, an elephantis of the sexual organs can occur. I had this very painful experience myself when I was in my early twenties. The vulva remained intensely swollen for days. I went to a doctor who had never seen anything like it. Similar to what guys call blue balls, women could shout a little louder about not getting off. We need our partners do the kind thing -- assist. I was too young to know better and was more interested in my partner's pleasure than mine. Cool baths with an orgasm will relieve this.

All humans are as different as night and day. We have different levels of sexual drive, or libido. Personal preference, mood, and sensitivity is exclusive to each individual. It seems a cruel joke that men want sex in the morning, while women's highest level of desire is reached at night. Men tend to want sex much more frequently than most women, causing several problems within relationships because of mismatched desire. It is no wonder that many opt for same sex relationships because the understanding of needs, timing, or desire is already innate.

An orgasm cannot happen for a woman if she is upset, the kids are screaming, or you have just told her that her ass is fat. Sex for women is over 80% mental.

Women need their head to be in the game, where men have a much more visual and physical experience. An orgasm cannot usually be achieved while hanging on. Surrender must happen to orgasm.

Pre-Mature Ejaculation - The Hair Trigger Penis (HTP)

Orgasm for men comes easily, often too easily. Pre-mature ejaculation occurs when a man spouts off prematurely. I have found from my own personal sexploration, that many men who come too quickly have deep-seated anger issues that need to be resolved. The hair-trigger of anger is a deep pattern that needs to be cleared which causes a hair-trigger penis. Neither are welcome at my tent. So do something about it, guys. It is curable. Get an energy clearing for your anger issues. I have helped many clients overcome these problems.

Over-Coming HTP - Pre-mature Ejaculation Without PORN

Men have been trained from boyhood to get off quickly. A hair-trigger response is the exact opposite of what women want and need. Pornography and self-pleasuring trains a quick response and pre-mature ejaculation. News flash! Women don't make love the way porn stars do. For those who have never watched pornography, a typical pornographic movie goes something like this:

Camera pans across an office building. A buxom blonde in a tight-fitting and low-cut red dress walks into an office in stiletto heels and reports for an interview. She sits in the waiting room nervously crossing her long legs, which reveal a sexy thigh. The camera pans her body from head to toe, slowly moving across her ample breasts and cleavage. She licks her glossy red lips as if she is licking a penis. A man clad in a suit with suspenders greets the young woman then invites her into his office. He asks her if she has ever had any office experience. She smiles and begins to disrobe. Within minutes his pants are being unzipped while she is going down on him under his desk.

Cut to the next scene, where the young woman is spread eagle on his desk with him pumping her from behind. This is pornography. No preamble, no relationship, just lots of women pleasuring men.

Just as the world is filled with all kinds of people there are many different ways to experience sex. Carnal desire is different for everyone. When we are young disconnected sex without love may be fun and exciting. Considered bumping uglies, today some experience frequent exchanges with many different partners to fulfill an emptiness or addiction. Disconnected sex is not the way to find true love or fulfillment. In my mind it creates more disconnection and can also create shame for women.

As I have gotten older, I have lost all interest in recreational sex with strangers that is void of emotion and spiritual connection. I find more enjoyment having a root canal, reading a good book, or walking out in nature. Real sex to me includes human involvement and connection. I prefer a friendship with my man first. I like to get to know him well, understand and know that I like him as a person, before I pursue a deeper, physical intimate experience. I knew my last partner for two years prior to having sex with him. Everyone is different. I am slow to allow someone in after having made uneducated choices in the past. I want to be sure I am seeing the real person before we have sex. I want authenticity, openness, and honesty. Not everyone is looking for this. These are my recommendations for a healthy balanced relationship rather than just a passionate sexual encounter.

My idea of deep connected sex encompasses a caring relationship, conversation, romance, anticipation, eye contact, kissing, connection, all over body massage, feather-light caressing and holding one another while enjoying each other's bodies and skin-to-skin contact. I like a slow build over months, where we might bump an elbow, or touch each other's arm. Call me old fashioned, but I have experienced the rip-each-other's-clothes off passion in the past. It was exciting. I enjoyed the pleasure, it was right for where I was emotionally.

Once you begin to love and respect yourself, your choices change. You move more slowly rather than jump into the sack. You recognize that being naked with someone is a sacred act. You want your partner to experience every inch of your body as an art-lover would examine a painting. I want someone to look into my eyes and show his love for me, rather than contempt for women. An exchange of laughter and play, imagination, ingenuity, and fun are involved. With emotional maturity, sex changes and evolves. My sense is it becomes more beautiful the older we get, because we know who we are and love what we have become. We become wiser, more deliberate, and careful with our choices. Some of us have a checkered past, that has become part of who we are. The colors of our past create the tapestry of our lives. We bring this tapestry with us everywhere. It needs to be accepted by the other first before we can allow them into our beds, hearts and lives.

Pounding at the Speed of Light

For some, sex is just about fucking. Getting off may be all that is required. From a quickie of 10 minutes or less, some never grow beyond the fast-paced train engine pounding at the speed of light. For most women, however, this type of sex falls short. It leaves a lot to be desired for the majority of women who require time to warm up, awakening the body-mind. For most women, great sex involves slow, methodical sensuality. Making love to each part of your partner's body, rather than only focusing on the target—the vagina. Imagine a rubber band around your wrist and each time you move to the vulva first. That rubber band needs to snap your wrist. We are re-training you to learn how to be a lover, rather than a fucker. Anyone can fuck. It takes an artist to make love. It takes patience, respect, and great communication with intimacy to be an amazing lover.

Growing Up is Hard to Do

It is unfortunate in this day and age when we are

inundated with sex on billboards, commercials, or television. We have become blasé´ about sex. Rather than making sex special, it has taken on a connotation of being degrading, and often guilt-ridden for women and teens. Girls are made fun of when they are virgins at school. My daughter was. It horrified me. This shows that parents don't educate their teens and young adults how to love and respect themselves or how to make love. Most parents don't discuss the difference between just getting off and lovemaking. It is a rarity for parents to spend time talking about sex with their teens, yet it is such a large part of their thought process. Their hormones are raging, often masturbating several times a day in many cases. A key step in development is missed. Kindness, respect, and tenderness are not part of the teenage scene. They see sex portrayed in video games, television shows, or on the Internet as pornography, not love-making. Many times boys grow into men without ever changing their style of lovemaking. Their sexpression does not mature with their mind and body. Which means by the time they marry, there has been no change in style, speed, or control of ejaculation. These men have no clue how to bring a woman to orgasm. They are not taught to care about it.

Men need to learn how to control and slow down ejaculation by using breath-work, visualization and changing up thrusting at one fast speed. Women need different speeds, angles with enough time to be able to reach the level of enjoyment that many male counterparts experience so quickly.

Nail Biting -
Holding Off an Impending Orgasm for Guys

Changing positions frequently can slow down a man's excitement level. Stopping and performing oral sex in between thrusting can raise a woman's enjoyment exponentially, while slowing down a man's orgasm. When the man thrusts and stops to perform oral sex, then goes back to thrusting, then back to performing oral sex, this can be an amazing experience for a woman. The first time that I had a g-spot orgasm was doing this very thing. So go back and read it again, you might have missed something.

Pornography is based on a man's fantasy of what sex is—it is not real lovemaking. It is base and child-like in nature. Most women want to have their body played with like an orchestra. An orchestra has wind instruments, strings, and percussion—not just one instrument. Our bodies have many different areas that can be stimulated so we can have an all-over body orgasm. Have fun, change positions, then make sex last longer than two minutes. Pornography fixates on the genitals. Amazing sex involves the whole body: breasts, nipples, hands, feet, neck, inner thighs, ears, fingers, and toes. Our skin is our biggest organ. Instead of showering separately before making love, begin in the shower. Soap on the vulva can burn and dry out the mucous membranes, so avoid using it. Stroke each other in the shower before you begin in the bedroom. Or take a bath together, without bubbles, paint her toenails. There are so many things that you can do that take sex "out of the box," so to speak.

Slowing down your breathing, changing positions

while moving your excitement from just your genitals to all over your body will help to take the pressure off your penis. Deep breathing with relaxation can help you move the energy to cycle it through your body instead of allowing the focus to be just on your genitals. Close your eyes while breathing into the sexual energy and pull it up into your heart. Envision it moving up, spreading throughout your entire body, neck, arms, legs, and feet. This way you begin to make LOVE with your heart instead of just your genitals. This will change your sexual experience from just a fuck to a magnificent experience for you both.

Changing Your Focus

Changing the way you make love, can change your pattern in a matter of months. Kissing, feather-light touching (as I have described for women) will help move your energy to flow all over your body, rather than focusing on just your penis or coming. When you take the emphasis off the end result - orgasm then focus on the act of lovemaking, you will not be so driven to come. Holding back your orgasm with breath, movement, you envision the energy spreading throughout the body. This relieves the build-up of energy in the penis, helping you last longer. Women need you to go slowly at first, building, stroking, kissing, sucking, and massaging. Changing it up with different types of touch and kissing focuses instead on your partner. This increases their pleasure instead of entirely focusing on yourself. Giving to the other person can help you contain, then release the pressure allowing more time between excitement and orgasm. Women don't just want to be pumped a few times till you get off, tossed aside while you drool all over your pillow snoring. Yes, we've seen you. Don't deny it.

Men often blame women for pre-mature ejaculation issues. I was married to someone who made me responsible for his problem. He had serious issues with rage. He finally got some help, but too late for our marriage. Can you imagine being married to someone for over 30 years, having him last only two minutes before he has an orgasm? Pre-mature ejaculation is a far greater issue than erectile dysfunction. It does not go away unless you get help or re-train yourself.

Pre-mature ejaculation is a very frustrating issue. It is a sexual dysfunction—one that leads to arguments with resentment on both sides. Pre-mature ejaculation is not caused by having sex too infrequently. It is not caused by not getting head. Nice try guys! I have heard it all. It will not get better on its own as you get older, either. Come on guys! Take ownership of your beautiful penis. Do some anger management or acupuncture therapy to remedy this. Call me and get an energy clearing series to remedy this issue. I clear the unconscious issues that created it in the first place. You have alternatives. There are many ways you can heal this without surgery, medication, or discomfort. Fix your little hair-trigger problem! Don't blame the women.

Make sex a whole body experience. Slow down your breathing and change positions often. Don't continue to pretend this is not a problem. Do something about it. Doing kegel exercises will help to strengthen your erection, help to remedy pre-mature ejaculation and also help prevent erectile dysfunction. Kegel exercises of the pubococcygeus (PC) muscles strengthen the pelvic floor and can help with urinary incontinence in both men and women later in life. Kegels are very beneficial for everyone, for different reasons. Exercise is good for everyone. Squeeze those PC muscles!

Foreplay is Not a Four-Letter Word!

For many women, they are able to receive pleasure, but getting all the way to orgasm seems like an impossibility. Without foreplay for most women, there is no orgasm. Foreplay is not an option. It is interesting: I read one sex book that poo-pooed foreplay. Naturally, it was written by a man. Men don't need foreplay.

If you want your woman to reach orgasm it is MANDATORY for the majority of women. If you are not receiving foreplay, it is time you did. Ask for it. Stop the presses! Whoa, lone ranger! You've gotta do your time, if you wanna spend your dime. Men will push our heads into their crotch to "hint" at what they want. Close your legs, look him in the eye and say, "Hey baby, I want you to go down on me first. You probably didn't realize how much I like it, I actually come that way." Tell him/her what you want. Practice, practice, practice. Get to know what feels good and what feels amazing!

When it comes to vaginal entry don't worry about dryness, use a quality lubrication product initially. However, the more sex you have the better lubricated you will be. If your vulva and vaginal cavity is tender, have more frequent sex with a good lubricant. There is a list of excellent lubricants in Chapter 9. Or have your hormones checked by a good lab, I have resources in the back of the book. If your estrogen or estrodiol is low, you may have vaginal tenderness.

I love sex. Yet in all my sexual escapades, (not on ice skates) most men hands down, try to skip or forego the act of foreplay. I can see a bumper sticker for men now: "FOREGO FOREPLAY!" I wonder if they knew what it felt like to go for years without an orgasm if they would continue to forgo this quintessential part of lovemaking and sex. Remember the experiment with Pavlov and his dog? Every time Pavlov rang a bell he gave his dog a treat. Pretty soon the dog learned when the bell rang he got a treat. Very quickly the dog began to salivate as soon as the bell rang.

This makes me wonder how I can ring a bell during this book, and re-train men to make foreplay as important as getting head? You might begin to salivate so get your napkin or towel ready. Ding! Foreplay! Ding! Head! Ding! You will love performing foreplay on your partner. Ding! You will love to perform foreplay on your lover. Ding! You will perform foreplay for at least twenty or even forty minutes on your lover and bring her to orgasm before you plunge any further! Ding! My hypnotherapy is coming in "handy!" Pun intended. Are you salivating yet?

Oral sex for forty minutes may make you a little fatigued. We care about you and your well being. We want our partners to keep their energy up. So why not try a vibrator? You will find that you are The Man when you show up with a handy little vibrating toy. When you can bring your woman to orgasm with ease and without breaking a sweat you will love that little hummer! Anything that makes you look and feel good, at the same time as your partner is a great little tool. Buy one for her as a surprise.

Author's Note:
I must note here, that using a vibrator on one person and then thinking you can use it on another will get you thrown out on your proverbial ass! Do not share a vibrator from one person to another due to bacteria, yeast, and other diseases. Buy a new one, keep it clean.

Many men use a little spit on the end of their penis - then push and plunge away. Their desire is to get into the soft pinkness of the vagina with a quickness, leaves us wondering what happened here? The problem is that women need moisture. Women need manual stimulation to have an orgasm. Just the word sex, is not enough to get women turned on to the point of penile insertion. Women's energy must be raised in preparation for sex. We are like the slow cookers or crock pots versus the fast fry of a man's rapid-fire arousal. We need appreciation, conversation, kissing, massage, and stroking. The "10 Minute Rule" (of "O" - my addition) for women according to my dear friend Ray Mastsen, is as follows;

• 10 minutes of kissing.
• 10 minutes of stroking, feather-light touch, kissing and attention to the breasts, inner thighs, buttocks, lower back and neck.
• 10 minutes of massage.
• 10 minutes of oral sex.

Do the math. That adds up to 40—count'em—minutes of stimulation. The last 10 minutes during oral sex, add the insertion of a finger gently, and just slightly inserted and pulled out stimulating the upper vaginal wall. Repeat. Between twenty and thirty minutes of stimulation the G-spot will be in evidence.

Ripp Torn

Without being sexually stimulated sufficiently, the sensitive tender tissue of the vagina can tear. If a woman says it hurts. Stop. Ask if you need more lubrication. Do not ignore her when she says it hurts. I had one man push forward anyway, even after I told him three times "it hurts!" When he called me afterward telling me he loved me, I gave him an ear full. You can't possibly love someone if you ignore them when they tell you they are in pain. If you push forward when your woman has told you that the sex hurts you are a beast without a heart. Stop. Ask her what she needs. Find another way to complete the sex act without hurting her, if you must. A hand job would be a good substitute.

Once a woman has a tear, penetration can be excruciating. After intercourse the tear can easily get infected or burned with urine. Tearing needs to be avoided. The way that it is avoided is through manual stimulation or foreplay with lubrication.

Vulvodynia - Vaginal and Vulvar Pain

There is also a condition that one in four women experience which causes intense vaginal and vulvar pain.

It is called Vulvodynia. My sense is that the source is from lack of self-love and self-acceptance. I am not an expert on this subject, although I can speak from personal experience. When I had Fibromyalgia, I experienced intense shooting pain through the vulva into the pelvic floor. When I finally loved and accepted myself completely, the pain from the Fibromyalgia stopped, as did the vulvar pain. I cannot stress the importance of self-acceptance with self-love. Often our programs and patterns of self-loathing are so deep that we are not aware. Molestation in childhood is often the source, but not always.

The Donut Hole on the Concession Stand of Life

Women need more stimulation than the in-out of a penis or tongue in our vagina to reach an orgasm. Target practice is what I call it when a sexual partner bypasses personal interaction as well as lips, breasts, inner thighs, skin, and zeros in on the clitoris and vaginal opening.

Women have so many wonderful body parts to stimulate. This heightens our pleasure centers, which would assist with arousal. Take your time and focus on each one for ten minutes. Instead of rushing to the finish line like a linebacker on Superbowl Sunday, slow down, you stallion! Great lovers take their time, but don't rush pleasure. Anticipation is key to heightened pleasure. Faster is not better—vary speed with pressure, try different things.

Getting a man to change his style of lovemaking may be gradual. Give him encouragement when he does something that feels good. However, some people don't listen. If they don't listen outside the bedroom, they won't listen inside the bedroom either. No one knows better what you need than you. So find out what you like. Practice makes perfect. Practice, practice, and more practice. Try it like Dr. Seuss. You will like it in your car, and you will like it on a star. Say, what a wonderful lover you are!

The problem is that most women have no idea what feels good because they don't feel comfortable exploring their own bodies. One of the things that I teach my coaching clients is self-stimulation. You would be surprised at how many women have never masturbated.

Most men feel completely comfortable stimulating themselves to orgasm. They do so regularly, whether they have partners, wives or not. Women need to explore their own bodies. Doing so will help you recognize what areas need to be stimulated to bring on a great orgasm. Self-stimulation will help your body open up and assist you if you want to come on a regular basis. When you self pleasure whether with a digit or a vibrator, you have the amazing opportunity to feel different sensations. You decide what you like or where you want it to happen, in just the right time.

Some people like having their anus stimulated. The anus is loaded with sensitive nerve endings. 61% of women have tried anal sex. According to Devi Ward, author, Tantric teacher, and former monk, there are eleven types of orgasms that a woman can have. An anal orgasm is only one of them. As a matter of fact, even with a vaginal orgasm some women also experience an anal orgasm whether the anus is stimulated or not.

The rising energy that surges from the anus to the brain is kundalini energy. It travels up the spinal column through the body, which culminates in the brain. Not only is a sexual experience pleasurable, it also releases tension and stress from the body. Sex does a body good!

Chapter Six
Sex As Medicine

Blake said that the body was the soul's prison unless the five senses are fully developed and open. He considered the senses the 'windows of the soul. When sex involves all the senses intensely, it can be like a mystical experience.
—Jim Morrison

NOT ONLY IS SEX fun, it relieves stress, improves the cardiovascular system, lowers blood pressure, and gives the body a full work out. Why spend hours at the gym sweating with a bunch of strangers when you could be sweating with the one you love?

As a matter of fact, a study performed by Queens University in Belfast tracked 1,000 middle-aged men over a ten-year period. The study found that men who reported the highest frequency of orgasm lived twice as long as though who did not enjoy sex. These findings are contrary to the tantric and Chinese teachings that ejaculation reduces a man's chi (energy), thereby shortening his life.

Prolong Life

Men who have sex twice a week have been reported to live 50% longer than men who are not having sex at all. Regular ejaculation actually is a great fun way to prevent prostate cancer in men, when self-acceptance and self-love is in place. Prostate cancer has been linked to feelings of frustration, sexual conflict, and unworthiness. I have found there is always an emotional component to disease. Traditional Chinese doctors support this theory. When you heal the emotional component, the disease is healed as well.

Sex improves circulation, lowers cholesterol and tones the pelvis, buttocks, stomach and arms. The heartbeat rises from 70 to 150 beats per minute, improving respiration, oxygenation, and mood. People who regularly enjoy sex are half as likely to have heart attacks and strokes as those who don't have sex at all.

Pain Relief - Headache Be Gone!

Orgasm is also a great pain reliever. I stopped taking pain medication over fifteen years ago. Orgasm is the best remedy for migraine headaches I ever found. Sex relieves the stress that restricts blood vessels in the brain. For those of you who say, "Honey, I've got a headache!" That reason just doesn't cut it anymore. Why not stimulate yourself to orgasm or have your partner stimulate you to orgasm instead and use your excuse not to, as a reason to enjoy sex.

Orgasm is a natural pain blocker, reducing pain up to fifty percent. Taking over-the-counter pain medication can have long-term side affects, which can cause kidney and liver damage. Orgasm has no such warning label. As a matter of fact regular sex will tone your abdominal muscles faster than doing crunches or push-ups and will put a smile on your face while you get buffed and fluffed (except at the point of orgasm when your face may be contorted).

Stress Relief

Stress is one of the leading causes of death. It contributes from 75% to 90% of all medical conditions, according to The Centers of Disease Control. Stress is the underlying cause of the six leading causes of death. Our thoughts or reactions to stressful situations is what causes our stress, rather than the situations themselves. How one person reacts to a situation could be totally different for someone who has a daily S&M routine (Sex and Meditation, not sadomasochism). Spiritual practice can keep you present, grounded and help you stay calm as well. It is a known fact that muscle tension is released upon orgasm. Sex is ten times more effective than valium for relaxing and relieving stress in the body. Sleep comes so much faster after enjoying the satisfying, rhythmic contractions of an orgasm. Because orgasms relieve stress, you will sleep deeper. Your sleep can be much more restorative, resulting in many health benefits.

Natural Opiates

An orgasm activates the same part of the brain—the anterior cingulate cortex and the insula—as pain. endorphins are released during sex with orgasm. They are the feel-good hormones (natural opiates of the body) that are released through a strenuous workout, or from sexual activity.

Neurons Get Excited Too

Endorphins flood the space between nerve cells and inhibit neurons from firing. Therefore sexual activity releases endorphins, which act as an analgesic for the body. These endorphins are a natural pain reliever. We get excited during sex, but so do our neurons. Excited neurons lead to an amazing feeling of well being. Well-being is a good thing. When we feel good, our thoughts are more positive. Our outlook on life is brighter. Depression is also relieved through sex. Now here is my prescription for those with anxiety, depression or stress; JUST DO IT! Get yours, then have some fun while getting healthier and extending your life.

Humans need skin to skin contact. An experiment was done during WWII on newborn infant children. Housed in a special facility the babies were scrupulously attended to. They were fed, kept clean, but no eye contact or touch other than what was required to feed and change them. Within four months half of the infants died. Even those that were rescued died shortly afterward. Although all the babies were physically healthy, they stopped verbalizing before their death no longer attempting to engage their caregivers. Sadly these babies did not even cry.

I mention this because I know many women who turn away from their husbands yet continue to boast about being married for twenty, forty, fifty or more years. Many women stop touching their husbands or even snuggling with them. Yet, say they are still married. I ask you, what is the point of continuing to stay married to someone that you don't touch, or even stopped making love to twenty or thirty years ago? It is inhumane, cruel, and insensitive to ignore each other's physical and emotional needs in this way. Withholding love, tenderness, touch, and affection is negative, insensitive behavior. A meaningful look, a tender touch on the arm, hand, or shoulder can mean so much to those you love. If you love them, let them know it rather than holding in your loving feelings. Life is far to short, let go of the resentment in your heart, and forgive instead.

Extra Virgin

Regular sex keeps you better lubricated and the soft vaginal tissue more flexible and less tender. Sex once a month or less does not give the body the ability to remember what it is supposed to do. You can find your tissue more prone to tearing, which is extremely painful. I recommend a natural lubricant to begin with rather than waiting until you have a tear. I recommend the use of extra virgin olive oil. I love the silky slippery way it feels. It adds so much to the experience. It does not burn like synthetic lubricants can. I have used it and returned to my virginal state! Isn't that what the extra virgin means?

With sex, you also receive the added bonus of the body's daily requirement of twelve daily hugs, an orgasm, pain reliever, as well as an all-over rush of happy hormones! Make love your drug! (It will not cause diabetes, heart disease, kidney failure, acid reflux, depression, anxiety, or heartburn.)

Endorphins will be released which you remember, excite your neurons, help you think more clearly, positively and improve your memory. Regular sex also prevents Alzheimer's and dementia because of the hormones that flood the brain. These feel-good hormones make a person feel euphoric, or high, naturally. Endorphin levels increase when a person exercises, goes into labor, or is stressed out.

Sex is a natural anti-histamine. It helps combat asthma and hay fever keeping the nose and airwaves clear. (Running out of excuses yet?)

Immune Boost

Kissing releases oxytocin and boosts our immune system. A kiss helps perpetuate attachment, can help you make-up, as it sends a message to the brain. Swapping spit with another person can reduce stress, help you relax and unwind. Yes, kissing is a stress reliever. It also boosts your immunity to certain diseases. Kissing encourages saliva production that encourages food to wash from the teeth. It also lowers acidity in the mouth that causes tooth decay. Believe it or not, kissing actually burns calories; up to twenty-five if you make out for more than a minute. Kiss her long enough to turn her on, and she may begin to have vaginal contractions and become wet. Wet with sex is good!

Gentle relaxed lovemaking reduces the chances of suffering from dermatitis. Sweating while lovemaking also helps to wash out pores and clears blemishes and makes the skin glow.

For those women who are still unconvinced that sex is good for you, sex helps keep you looking young. A study performed by the Royal Edinburgh Hospital in Scotland by a panel viewed participants through a one-way mirror. The women who looked between seven to twelve years younger were enjoying lots of sex (up to four times a week). One of the reasons noted for these women looking "super young" is that sex increases estrogen levels which normally wane with age. Estrogen helps to keep your hair looking shiny, with skin supple and glowing. A smile instead of a frown on your face doesn't hurt either. Naturally formed estrogen is much safer for the body than taking hormones, botox, or a facelift. Sex hormones also affect the parathyroid and growth hormone production, which helps to maintain bone-density and firmer more youthful skin.

To recap, below is a list of all the health benefits of regular sex:

1. Lowers blood pressure.
2. Reduces risk of heart attack.
3. Reduces risk of stroke.
4. Reduces stress levels.
5. Enhances mood.
6. Relieves depression.

7. Is a natural pain reliever.

8. Gives the body an all-over work-out. The equivalent of a 30 minute work-out.

9. Increases cardiovascular circulation.

10. Increases oxygenation of the blood.

11. Increases longevity.

12. Fights colds and flu by improving immune system.

13. Burns calories.

14. Regular sex keeps you looking young, beautiful and radiant

15. Puts a smile on your face.

16. Enhances your relationship.

17. Increases Intimacy

18. Couples that have regular sex have happier lives and a lot more fun together.

19. Keeps menstrual cycles regular.

For those of you who often are, "not in the mood," isn't it time to get that stick out of your ass, get some, increase your lifespan, and improve your bitchy mood?

Chapter Seven
Love That Lasts

I am not saying renounce sex, I am saying transform it. It need not remain just biological: bring some spirituality to it. While making love, meditate too. While making love, be prayerful. Love should not be just a physical act; pour your soul into it. —Osho

SEX IS NOT JUST about "getting some." Sex is also about giving. Often in the process of giving we get turned on. Sometimes we are so co-dependent that we give from a place of emptiness, then feel resentful for giving. We have to be fully empowered as an individual to contribute fully in a relationship.

Go with the Flow

Bliss is joy. Enjoy life as a wonderful experience of little Blissful events and being open to receive. When we are open and let go of control we allow all the possibilities to show up on our doorstep.

The happier we are with ourselves, the more positive experiences occur. Blessing our partners, being kind and loving all day every day rather than just when it comes time to have sex, is key. Life is one big orgasm when you enjoy whatever happens. Each day can be blissful when we wake up being grateful to be alive. The more positive and loving of ourselves, the more positive and loving and accepting of others we are.

Equality and Power

The happiest couples have equality within the relationship. Power is spread evenly while both parties are perfectly able to live singly if the need arises. Neither is dependent on the other or is happy alone. The relationship is the icing on the cake. Rather than the relationship is everything. When a relationship becomes more important than the individual, a pattern of giving too much while losing one's self occurs. It is important to retain integrity of self, rather than giving up your soul for a relationship. When you give up friends, family, or even a job to make your partner happy, eventually one or both of you will become resentful. You may recognize that you have lost yourself along with your own way. This is often when one party will leave the other saying they need to find themselves. They gave too much, because they did not love themselves enough to develop, then set and implement healthy boundaries. One rushed home, while the other went to the gym. One became a home body while the other became embroiled in a life outside of the marriage. There needs to be balance. Doing things together, like travel, vacations and activities that are fun. Not just the drudgery of work, kids and sleep.

Sex is the Glue - Not the Foundation

Sex for the average healthy couple in a long-term committed relationship or marriage often becomes dull and ordinary. It takes time, effort, creativity, and devotion to keep sex passionate, but also exciting. Many people put their love life on the back burner after just a few years, downplaying its importance. Having time each week for fun, dinners out with a chance to talk and reconnect is imperative for the longevity of the relationship or marriage. The relationship is important, but neither party should give up everything for the other, either. A healthy balance is required.

Communication needs to occur on a daily basis. Honesty, integrity, and authenticity are what build intimacy. Deep profound intimacy includes regular conversations that are meaningful, being present while listening to one another. Conflicts need to be resolved quickly rather than dragging on for days. Yelling at one another, name-calling, abuse, or sarcasm have no place in a balanced healthy relationship. Blame and victimization are also not productive.

An equitable distribution of power within the relationship is imperative for the longevity of a marriage or partnership. When one person holds all the power and dictates how the household is run, the other is left feeling disempowered and impotent. Oftentimes when one person wields the power, there is an air of fear or control. A relationship needs to be a loving partnership void of fear.

My personal experience growing up was one where my father held the purse strings and dolled out money to my mother. Although they disciplined us children together at times, intimacy was missing between them. I feel that was due to my father's rage.

In one of my marriages, rage, control and fear figured prominently. Interestingly enough he was the same husband who told me I had a fear of intimacy. Was my fear of him, or rather intimacy? I was terribly afraid of him. When we are afraid of our partners, it is difficult to allow them close. Each time a wall is punched, or we are threatened physically, a piece of love is chipped away, never to return. When we live in an abusive household, it feels like walking on eggshells, which creates uncertainty. We never know when rage or anger will erupt. Rage, low self-esteem and abuse go hand-in-hand. They do not allow closeness or real love in because of the underlying patterns of unworthiness, and abuse.

The sharing of power is what leads to deep and lasting intimacy. Friendships outside of the relationship allow each partner to express emotions outside of the marriage or partnership—lessening the emotional dependence on the partner. Feeling that you only need one person in your life places a huge amount of pressure on the partnerships instead of spreading the need for emotional support within a network of friends.

When one person gives up too much of themselves, core values are compromised. Accommodating too much can also create resentment. Intimacy is more important now than ever, meaning that relationship equality has become more important. In each relationship, partners have ups and downs. We pick up the slack for each other in these times. To think that a division of power can be perfect is to say that there is a perfect relationship, which only happens in Disney movies.

Adventures in Monogamy

There are many advantages to monogamy. As trust builds, intimacy deepens. Sex can improve as two people get to know each other through the exchange of ideas, thoughts, and dreams. With good communication about preferences and desires exchanged outside of the bedroom, connection between couples deepens. You take your love and lovemaking to a higher level. Sex becomes an art form, one of sensual pleasure with bliss for both parties. As connection and trust build, an openness to explore different options like dressing up in sexy lingerie while doing a strip tease a la, Nine And A Half Weeks might ensue. Nothing is off-limits unless you mutually decide it should be. Being creative with lovemaking can help keep your love alive and your relationship strong. More often than not, couples fall into the trap of cursory quickies, which usually satisfy the man, but rarely give the woman what she needs.

Life happens, bills pile up and children are born. The stress of work, raising a family coupled with the issues of finances takes a toll on intimacy and relationships. The best marriages continue to have regular lovemaking sessions, rather than quickies as a steady diet. Instead of having sex several times a week, most couples begin to fall into the pattern of sex once a week or even less than once a month. Most normal healthy men require sex more than three times a week well into their 40s. From the men I interviewed most report that they could have sex every day with the "right" woman. Women's desire rarely matches the sexual appetites of their partners, causing resentment, anger, or other issues within the marriage.

Burned Out and Turned Off

Sometimes, the attraction for a new person ignites a latent passion that has not been felt in years. Unfortunately, many couples are opting to have affairs because the home fires are no longer burning. One or both parties long for the flush and excitement of a new person. Staying faithful and committed to one person creates trust, and opens you up to deep intimacy. This also creates a depth of expanded love that cannot be present when one or both parties have affairs. Sexually transmitted diseases are passed onto the unsuspecting partner. Secrets cannot remain hidden forever; the truth eventually comes out. Depending on the foundation or commitment to stay together, 37% manage to work out their differences after an affair. Getting over the betrayal of an affair will take a toll on trust. The injured party has to let go to forgive. It takes a loving person with good self esteem to be able to repair the damage.

Affairs and Other Achilles' Heel

According to StatisticBrain.com, 57% of men admit to being unfaithful in any relationship, while 54% of women cheated. 36% admitted to infidelity with a co-worker, with 35% of men and women having affairs on business trips. Most affairs last an average of two years. Time, energy, and love is being channeled in a different direction and undermines the marriage. 74% of the men surveyed said that they would have an affair if they thought they could get away with it, while 68% of women would. It is easy to have an affair. The question is, is it worth the devastation it causes? Sex is fleeting. Trust takes time to build. With one short affair, trust is eliminated. Thinking that you can get away with something is arrogant. You may never get back to the place you were before the affair. A short-term titillation can devastate a family. Children become the casualty of someone's lack of character and self-control. Children of divorce are less likely to have successful marriages if they marry at all. They are more likely to commit crimes, rape and have emotional issues than children of couples who remain together. They are also more likely to drop out of school, take drugs, overdose, and commit suicide. Careful consideration must be given to your responsibilities when you lust after someone outside of your marriage. Perhaps you are thinking or having an affair to avoid reality, responsibilities, and recognizing your life is not what you wanted it to be. Yet, the short-term excitement will hurt many. Even children who are not consciously aware of the affair are damaged psychologically. Anger surfaces long after the affair is over.

Most people think that they can get away with an affair. Three of my husbands had them and I knew each time. Even without evidence, there is an energy that is felt by the one left at home. Circumstances will arise that will bring the truth to the surface. If you are thinking you can get away with it, think again. There are those, however, that allow the evidence to be brushed under the carpet. They would rather allow the affair than lose the marriage.

Lies become the norm, while subterfuge consumes the trust and honesty that was once present. The newness of making love to someone you don't know, versus the one you know too well can make an affair seem justified. Many feel that their spouse is not giving them the attention they deserve in the bedroom or elsewhere. Children become the priority. Men feel left out, ignored, or less important than the new baby. Many women suffer from post-partum depression, lowered libido, or even low self-esteem that can last for years. Other women become enraptured with their newborn child leaving their husband feeling left out in the cold. While men are out in the workplace, their attention is often caught by sexy, flirty women whose bodies are not misshapen from childbirth. A little flirtation from a woman who listens, pays attention, or turns them on, can make a man feel vindicated for satisfying his sexual urges. As my aunt Margaret, a medical doctor, used to say, "A standing cock has no conscience," which means once a penis is erect, men think with their penis-brain rather than with the brain in their head. Due to the blood flow re-directed to the penis, the brain takes a hiatus. Only one brain can operate at a time. While the main brain is on hiatus, the penis has a will of its own.

Science proves this point as well in a 2008, study done by *The Journal Of Evolutionary Society* found that men in the mere presence of women acted differently. They are more apt to take risks, jaywalk, wait to the last second to dash onto a bus. A 2011 paper published in the *Personality and Social Psychology Bulletin* says that just looking at women's faces or legs, whether in person or in pictures, would cause men to "induce mating goals." In plain English, viewing a woman causes a man to puff up like a mating peacock to attract the female. Men are more likely to take risks while playing blackjack, or disregard the future while making luxury purchases. Women on the other hand, are not affected a bit by men's risk taking, quick jumping on buses, or the purchase of expensive cars in order to impress us.

Author's note: One of my editors deleted the above paragraph calling it utter bullshit. Needless to say I fired his white ass!

It takes a strong person to remain committed, faithful and honest. It is much easier to have an affair than to remain faithful. Most men will stray eventually, if their sexual needs are not being met at home. Women too have affairs. Keeping your love life interesting and spicy will help to keep you both from yawning during sex. There are no guarantees that your relationship will last the test of time. Keeping sex interesting, exciting, and passionate will certainly help. Changing up your patterns from the time of day you have sex, to the positions you use adds variety and interest as well as excitement. When you perform sex the same way, week after week, anyone would become bored or lose interest. We change jobs, move houses, and then learn new skills. Lovemaking is a skill worth having.

Continuing to expect your partner to not be pleasured to orgasm is setting your relationship up for failure. It is a form of communication that emanates throughout the household or relationship. Those who remain attracted to their spouses have a better track record for fulfilling sex lives. Best selling author and former movie star, Marlo Thomas, was interviewed on the *Today* show in April, 2014. While talking about her new book, *It Ain't Over Till It's Over.* She was asked about the longevity of her 35-year marriage to talk show host, Merv Griffin. Marlo replied, "When the sex is good it is 35% of the relationship. When the sex is bad, it is 80% of the relationship." Static resentment, irritation, and other issues surface and become problematic. Sex does not solve problems, but rather is the cause of many when there is a disconnect or the couple is in disagreement about frequency and type of sex they engage in. Resentment outside the bedroom shows up in the bedroom.

I have found that stories teach better than narratives do. They also have a tendency to be more believable. You can see yourself in the character's place. When you can try on these scenarios yourself, you will learn new techniques with ways of making love that you had not considered before. I use stories to teach the philosophy of sex as an art form and lifeline to keep you healthy, fulfilled and balanced. Let's take a look at Marvin and Sarah's little tryst.

Sex In The Afternoon - Marvin and Sarah

Marvin shoots his wife a knowing look; they race up the stairs to the bedroom while the kids are out of the house. They have a full hour of peace, quiet and privacy. Sex is always better when they know the kids can't hear them. Marvin kicks off his running shoes, and leaves his socks on—his feet always get cold. Sarah slides her jeans over her hips and wriggles out of them. She kicks her underwear up into the air and quickly catches them and places her underwear with her jeans neatly on the bedside chair. She fumbles with the buttons of her silk blouse, ripping one off, "Damn!" She realizes that she has ripped the fragile silk under her button right in the middle of her ample breasts. Anywhere else and it would not be noticed. This was her favorite blouse. The color made her skin look warm and gave her a youthful glow. Everyone complemented her when she wore it.

She stomped angrily into the bathroom to pee. She could not shake the disappointment of ruining her blouse. She knew she could not replace it, even if they had the money to spend right now, which they didn't. She really didn't want to have sex; she had so much to do. She had other ways she preferred to spend an hour of her time when the kids were gone. She never had an orgasm and sex was perfunctory. After sixteen years they knew each other well. Marvin had kept himself in pretty good shape and her Pilates classes ensured that she remained pretty close to her college weight. She loved Marvin. He was a good provider and a good father. But sex, had become unimaginative—almost hollow. Even when it was wonderful it took her forever to come. It was a chore to reach orgasm, and try as she might, she rarely got there. It seemed like everything had to be perfect for her to reach anything close to an orgasm. If clitoral stimulation wasn't involved, orgasm didn't happen. Most often it was over almost as soon as it began.

Marvin climbed into the cold sheets and reached over to the bedside drawer for the bottle of lube. He opened the bottle and leaned over to Sarah as she plunked one knee onto the bed and began to lubricate her vulva and the outside of her vagina. Sarah pushed his hand away and exclaimed, "Can't you wait till I am in the bed?" She dutifully lay on her back and opened her legs, while Marvin knelt over her, preparing to enter her. Without so much as a kiss, Marvin climbed on top of Sarah and pushed his swollen penis into her dry vagina. He began to pump vigorously in and out of Sarah. She winced in pain, but Marvin was in full swing, his eyes closed. He had no idea how little sensation Sarah was able to feel, since she is not aroused and not fully lubricated. She couldn't go from zero to sixty like he could. The mere suggestion of sex gave Marvin a hard-on. "What I wouldn't give to be a man," Sarah thought.

She pinched her nipples in an attempt to arouse herself just in time to hear Marvin above her in the throws of orgasmic bliss. He rolled off her onto his side of the bed saying, "Oh my God! That was amazing. Did you come?" Sarah lowered here face and shook her head, "No." Today was like every other sexual encounter she had with Marvin. He was happy and she wasn't. Marvin kissed her on the cheek and threw a limp arm around her and pulled his wife close. He whispered in her ear, "I'll get you next time." Sarah had heard that promise before. Sometimes, she would go into the bathroom after Marvin fell asleep and sit on the toilet and masturbate or cry. Depending on her mood. She wished she knew how to change things. She and Marvin had a pretty good relationship. They didn't argue much, although there was tension when they weren't intimate. It seemed to really put him in a bad mood. Sometimes they would go for weeks and even months before she would let Marvin get near her. She just wasn't that interested. Sarah felt that Marvin was only using her as if she was a receptacle, any port in the storm. She didn't like that feeling and it plagued her. If he was left high and dry almost every time they had sex, like she was, Sarah bet there would be some changes that was for sure. They just seemed out of synch. Marvin was ready four-to-five times more often than she wanted sex. Sometimes she just wished he would find another way, but not really. She didn't want a divorce. She was just ambivalent about sex. It wasn't that great. Frankly it left her cold, no more like really rare steak, just beginning to cook. Maybe that was why she wasn't more motivated to have sex. She gave him blowjobs when she wasn't in the mood. By the time Marvin was about to come she began to start getting revved up. Man, that was a pattern.

The issue with Sarah and Marvin is that Marvin is unconscious in his lovemaking. He is focused only on his own pleasure. He does not recognize that there is a disconnect. He receives, but doesn't give to Sarah. Sarah is resentful even before they begin to make love, because of past history. She rips a button off her shirt, and then blames Marvin silently. When Marvin grabs at her, like a teenage boy, Sarah is angry. Anger does not create a good energy for sex to be fulfilling for both parties. Sarah is clearly not being satisfied, while Marvin has a pattern of promising to "catch her later."

Sarah is not buying it anymore and is generally upset, resentful and becoming totally disinterested in sex. If Marvin and Sarah don't make some changes, with a sex coach or relationship coach, they could end up being a couple that stops having sex when they both hit 50. Marvin could become passive aggressive as could Sarah. Their communication is already poor. Without a physical outlet, it will only deteriorate further. Sarah needs to confront Marvin about her dissatisfaction in the bedroom to teach Marvin how to make love instead of just grope at her.

Chapter Eight
Sexual Healing

Healing doesn't mean the damage never existed.
It means the damage no longer controls our lives.

NOTHING LEAVES YOU FEELING more broken, dysfunctional, or left out than having sex for years without an orgasm. Yet for millions of women all over the world, orgasm continues to elude them. We have been damaged, raped, assaulted, and molested. All of these transgressions have left their toll. From frigidity to not wanting to have sex at all, sexual dysfunction can leave you feeling something is really wrong with you.

Shame, for many women, is a part of our long-standing issue. When we hold shame in our bodies, orgasm can be illusive. It is another layer that needs to be healed in order to fully step into our feminine power.

My Personal Healing - Tantra Style

I have been there myself. For years I had sex without orgasms, with partners who got frustrated and left, saying, "Its just not fun for me." My belief is the trauma remains in our DNA from one generation to the next. However, it can be cleared, healed, and remedied with patience, courage and a lot of guts. I knew I had all of those attributes, albeit a little shaky on the courage piece.

The fright, flight, or freeze response has been in our DNA since the dawn of creation. It used to help us run from dangerous animals. This response also occurs when a child is molested. The fear of the event remains frozen in our cells. I would not have believed this had I not experienced it personally.

Except for a couple of experiences, I did not have orgasms through vaginal sex without self-pleasuring, well into my 50's. While living in Atlanta, Georgia, I began to search for a Tantra class. I knew from my research that Tantra could help heal my issue. I found a group that was well known and began to follow their blog. I read about their work for well over a year. When I moved to Boulder, Colorado, I was determined that something would change. There was a group, puja experience (with clothes on,) that offered sacredness, devotion while honoring of both sexes. I attended this puja experience in Boulder bravely alone. I also attended several group gatherings becoming more comfortable in this setting. I also became more comfortable with the attendees. After three such gatherings I got up the nerve to attend a Tantra workshop. There I met at least eight Tantrikas, who did sexual healing. I had ample opportunity to talk to different practitioners, to find a couple I would feel comfortable with. After attending the advanced workshop, I went through a sacred sexual healing process with the couple I chose.

I had been married and divorced four times. What did I have to lose? I knew that I did not want to die without being able to step fully into my sexuality. I loved sex, but it wasn't complete without the ability to orgasm fully. I knew that being non-orgasmic was more than a sexual block—it was also emotional. Releasing it from the pelvic area is what is required to regain sexual function. Much of the trauma is frozen in the pubis bone, the sitz bones and the vagina cavity itself. Because the G-spot is so spongy, it absorbs and holds trauma as well.

Feeling safe is extremely important when it comes to sexual healing. I understood that through the sexual molestation, fear overcame me and was frozen in my vagina, thighs, and buttocks. The human body goes into fright, freeze or flight. When I was unable to run away, my cellular memory froze the fright deep inside. The process that was used, involved squeezing the muscles in the buttocks, pushing in on the sitz bones and gently massaging the inside of the vaginal walls and G-spot.

Most men would think that this experience was hugely sexual. I can assure you that during the procedure, sex and/or pleasure were the last things on my mind. On my first appointment, I met with the woman, who interviewed me about my past sexual experiences and my G-spot orgasm. When I had that experience, my boyfriend shamed me thinking that I peed on him. This further blocked my ability to orgasm. When my partner, John, died right after making love, this also was traumatic and scarred me. All of these traumas blocked my ability to let go and enjoy the pleasure than my partners enjoyed.

The second appointment was a two-hour appointment, with both of them present. Being heterosexual, I chose to have him do the healing, while she lay beside me, holding me. It was rather strange, because I felt intuitively that there was some judgment on her part, of me. My guidance told me I was in the right place while this was definitely the right timing.

I wore a sarong that I had purchased in Bali, Indonesia, to the treatment room. It helped me to feel safe and beautiful. I had to say—I felt more like a lamb going to slaughter than a Tantra client. The room was darkened, though it was 4:00 in the afternoon. Soft New Age music played in the background. Candles were lit, the room was clean and scented. A large beach towel neatly covered the bed. I was asked to disrobe for the healing. Lying on my back with my legs propped up on pillows the practitioner systematically massaged me. Every point that he touched felt like I was being seared with a red-hot poker. Although he was gentle, it was so intensely painful, that I wept. I am not a chicken. As a matter of fact, I am totally fearless. I did landscaping work for eleven years in high heat, humidity, and the frigid cold. There was little I would not do when I was motivated to do it. From laying sod to moving boulders, this was the most difficult thing I had ever experienced. I am a strong woman, fiercely committed to my healing. I wanted to leave. I wanted to give up. I kept holding my breath because of the intensity of the pain. The pain internally was the worst. There was absolutely no pleasure experienced. I could not have the intended orgasm at the end, due to the intensity of the pain.

Orgasm was the furthest thing from where my head or body was. I felt like I had failed. I wondered if the process was successful.

Two years later, I experienced oral sex with a partner. I took my time getting to know him. For over two years, we talked on the phone and saw each other on rare occasions. Finally, I knew it was time. I had not been intimate with a man for over two years. I had no idea what would happen.

My experience was amazing. Not only did I have an orgasm, I was filled with intense joy. Much to my amazement, I laughed throughout the entire experience. I did not fail; I had healed that deep part of me that had been frozen in time for so long. This is what I have come here to do, to show other women that they, too, can heal that part of themselves—that they, too, can experience joy. I had systematically cleared my energy, reached deep within, doing much introspection, and letting go. I knew that it was not just the work that I did with the Tantrikas that allowed my incredible orgasm to happen. The self-love that I had been teaching and guiding others through, was the emotional piece for me. I had truly let go of the past. What a huge relief.

What is the G-Spot?

The G-spot was originally named for Dr. Ernst Gräfenberg, who described a one to two centimeter area located approximately one to two inches inside, on the upper vaginal wall. In 1950, Dr. "G" set the wheels in motion for Western medicine to prove its validity. The *Kamasastra* and *Jayamangala* scripts dating back to 11th century India describe a similar sensitive area. It is located approximately, a thumb's length from the vaginal opening, although this varies from person to person. The G-spot is said to be the root of the clitoris, hence all those wonderful nerve endings and sensitivity. Not only were women gifted with the ability to reproduce, we also have the ability to squirt! When you think about it, that is one scary combination to bequeath one sex with.

Yes, every woman has a G-Spot. Each and every woman has this innate ability to have a G-spot orgasm AND squirt. The issue is that women so rarely get stimulated enough to get the G-spot activated. Once you have stimulated yourself to orgasm, that is the time to look for the G-spot. Looking before you have had an orgasm will be futile for most women, as it doesn't show its pretty head until you are turned on, as in VERY TURNED ON!

Where is the G-Spot?

Feel along the upper wall of the vagina, approximately an inch and a half to two inches north (towards the navel). It takes a contortionist to reach this area. Most women are unfamiliar with it, partly because the location is difficult to reach. Men rarely stimulate this area digitally because they have to turn their wrist upwards and reach inside with a bent finger, doing a come-hither motion. A G-spot wand will do the trick with less wrist and finger cramping. Focused attention on the G-spot will stimulate it, however, there are some additional facts you need to be prepared for.

The G-Spot must be the focus rather than just

thrusting a finger anywhere inside the vagina. Just as men have incredibly sensitive nerve endings along the underside as well as the tip of the penis, women have the G-Spot.

When a woman begins to get really aroused, this area will swell and feel ridged and spongy to the touch. The G-Spot is the size of a quarter, larger when aroused. If you are having difficulty locating the spot, place some pressure on the outside of the mons pubis (the hairy area above the pubic bone). Putting pressure on the outside while crooking your finger in the come-hither motion will do the trick. Remember, little Gina is a tricky little number. She hides until deep arousal takes place. If your partner has never had a G-spot orgasm it is because you have never spent enough time stimulating her. Not that she is incapable of it.

Usually, the G-Spot swells when a partner is just getting ready to have an orgasm inside her. As the gland (head) of the penis swells right before orgasm it begins to stimulate the G-Spot. As the G-spot is stimulated with the swelling penis, it too becomes swollen and engorged. The penis cannot contort enough (unless it has a crook in the middle) to reach the G-spot. Doggie style may be better, but you would have to pull back and almost out of the vagina, to reach it. Placing a pillow, wedge, or cushion under the female's buttocks tips up the pelvis allowing a better angle.

Female Prostate

The G-spot is the female counter-part to the male prostate. It is bean-shaped. When aroused, it feels spongy and rough, like a washboard dirt road.

G-Spot Sensitivity

For the women, you will know you have the right area because you will feel the urge to urinate. Get up, empty your bladder, and then try again. The urge to pee will diminish. Stay with it. Bear down slightly with a towel under your buttocks. Most women jerk or run in the other direction when this area is touched. Mostly because there is sexual trauma stored there. The first time the G-Spot is stimulated could be painful. If your partner has ever been molested, shamed for touching herself as a child, or traumatized sexually at all, this area will need some gentle, loving, pressure as well as healing touch. Breathe through it, rather than stop. It gets better, I promise.

Why Most Women Never Have a G-Spot Orgasm

Pain from trauma stays frozen in the G-Spot and has shut down this area. One in three women have been sexually molested, or abused globally. Often they don't even remember, as they were so young when it happened. Even shame from sexual touching in childhood can be enough to freeze pain in the G-Spot, brain, and thighs. I have been asked, why there is pain stored in the tops of the thighs. When you think about having sex with a woman, a man's body drapes across hers, resting his body on her thighs. When it is a child being molested, the act is frozen in the body parts where the most pressure, pain, or touch has been. If it hurts, most women don't want to continue with touch in this area. They will shun stimulation, avoiding the pain. Moving THROUGH the pain is what is needed. Until you heal the pain and trauma, there will be no G-Spot orgasm. The other side of pain is where the ultimate pleasure is. Stay with it, it is soooo worth it!

How to Heal the G-Spot Trauma

Professionally trained Tantrikas can help you heal this area. As a couple, this can be done in the privacy of your own home in a nurturing safe environment. If you are willing to heal this area on your own, know it is possible. Patience, caring and understanding are a must. The first time, old emotions, tears will probably surface and it could be excruciatingly painful.

Your partner needs to put some gentle pressure on the sitz bones first. These are the bones in the buttocks that you sit on. Hold, breathe, and release. Hold, breathe, and release again. The tops of the thighs also are a place where trauma is stored. Deep tissue massage here, with deep breathing will help. The legs store a lot of our trauma. Keep breathing deeply. Do not hold your breath, as this further shuts down this area. Maintain eye contact throughout as well.

Quantum Light Breath technique is a way to release the trauma with less discomfort than deep tissue massage. There will still be some deep tissue massage needed after doing the Quantum Light Breath as well. You may have to repeat the breathwork several times to completely release all the trauma. This is a free download from the Internet. You can also see a practitioner, like me for this type of healing in person.

Most people stop at this point. Committing to move through the pain to heal the trauma is a must. If the two of you agree to do this as a healing, know that orgasm is not the goal (during the healing process). Healing is. Let go of pressure, and work together to heal the area. Take as long as is needed to complete the process. You will probably need several sessions to get through all the way to orgasm after the trauma is released. Emotional sensitivity from your partner is needed to do this as a team. Keep eye contact. Stay connected; don't let your mind wander. You don't have to think about the past to release trauma. It comes out of the cells with the touch and deep tissue massage of the G-spot and legs.

Since most of us don't associate pain with intercourse, this is as far as most couples get. Speaking from experience, the pain was so intense I wanted to stop. I cried. I needed to take breaks and keep breathing. There was nothing sexual about the experience for me. It was too painful for it to be sexual. We tend to hold our breath when something hurts. That is the opposite of what we need. Remember to breathe and relax through the pain. Tensing only makes pain worsen. Remember you are releasing all that no longer serves you. Surrender to the process. Remind yourself this is worth it to let go of all the old pain. It is so worth it. Give yourself the time you need, cry, breathe, then begin again.

Keep breathing through this, it will pass. Go slowly. Gentle come-hither stroking with one or two fingers with the hand turned upward. Gently stroke this area, keeping eye contact through the process. Your partner must remind you to keep breathing.

Keep Eye Contact

Sexually traumatized women often disconnect during sex. It is imperative that you maintain eye contact to keep them present and connected through the process. With closed eyes they can disconnect and go somewhere else. Healing involves presence, rather than disconnection. Think of this as a healing only. If orgasm results it is a bonus. It may take two or three of these healing sessions to clear all that has been frozen in this area for years. Don't rush. Be patient. Believe me the benefits once this pain has passed, are so worth it.

G-Spot Wand

There are tools specifically created to reach the G-Spot. I caution you, however, as some are made of acrylic and can feel hard and too severe at first. The finger is gentler, until the pain diminishes. Use olive oil or coconut oil, relax, and breathe. Doing this on your own could be less stressful if your partner isn't up to the task. I recommend the G-spot wand either way.

Disappointment and Frustration

Women often end up frustrated because our needs

are in opposition to what a man needs. This is why you need to make sure you spend twenty minutes stimulating her body, neck, breasts, vulva, clitoris, vagina, and G-Spot individually. I mention vagina and G-Spot separately because the stimulation of each is different. Read the section in Chapter 5 before you throw in the towel or say, "Holy Hell!"

Frankly, it is an awkward spot to reach. It requires some stretching on your partner's part, but is so worth it when you do.

Female Ejaculation

Women have the ability to ejaculate just as men do. What comes out of a woman's vagina is not urine. Some men shame women the first time they experience this event, saying that she peed on them. Shame needs to be eliminated completely. If you shame your partner for an ejaculation, it may be her last one. You can create trauma by shaming her, further traumatizing her. What is emitted is ejaculate, similar to vaginal secretions or a man's ejaculation. Of course is does not contain seminal fluid, only men have the ability to carry sperm. If you are concerned about the spray, place a towel underneath you.

If ejaculation occurs, celebrate! This is a grand event. Think how you would feel if you never experienced ejaculation in your lifetime, most women never do. Remember, if you have been molested in the past, you need patience, kindness with love. If your partner can't give that to you, perhaps they aren't the right one?

An excellent depiction of healing sexual trauma was

made. This movie *Bliss* came out in 1987, with Craig Sheffer, Sheryl Lee and Terrence Stamp as the sex therapist (Tantra Master). I highly recommend this movie as it depicts the issues of sexually dysfunctional women and how one couple dealt with it. This movie is available on Netflix.

Women Come First, Last and Always!

It's been so long since I've had sex I've forgotten who ties up whom. —Joan Rivers

To pleasure a woman, you have to think like one. Romance opens a woman's heart. It is the key to opening her beautiful legs and allowing you in. We like to feel deeply connected to someone before we have sex with them. A phone call or text letting us know you are thinking about us during the day means so much. Bringing home flowers or a special book we have been talking about speaks volumes about how you feel about us. If you make it all about the sex, you will never win our hearts, consistency and selfless giving in the bedroom. Romance is the butter on the frying pan that keeps sex sizzling.

Childbirth and aging change our bodies. We become loose in places we want to be tight and tight in places we want to be loose. Our bodies are far from the perfection of a young girl's. We don't want to be told that we can lose that tummy, like one of my husbands told me. You try having three babies with c-sections and see what your stomach looks like! Put your head in ours. Each time you make a hurtful comment, it goes into our memory bank and chisels away at our love for you. If it feels like mistreatment a powerful woman will eventually leave. Powerful women want a man who can converse with her intelligently without trying to fix her or change her mind. We want to be accepted for who we are.

Sex needs to begin with the mind. Once you turn on a woman's mind, her imagination will begin to stir and run wild. With some romance, dinners out and to be told we are beautiful. We need to know that dinner was great if we cooked, or that our hair looks nice. If we have been working at losing weight and exercising at the gym, we need to know you notice. We all need to be noticed, appreciated, as well as accepted. We need to see your actions agree with what you are saying. Women have been lied to, cheated on and put down for hundreds of years. We need acceptance. Trust is built through getting to know someone. Without trust there can be no intimacy. Trust is the authentic feeling we have in the presence of a person that our body senses is safe. Trust stimulates oxytocin. Oxytocin is also released when we have sex with someone. Having sex too early can make us feel trust for someone we shouldn't. I know I have beaten that dead horse, flogged it, reminded you, yet again.

Women need the mood to be set, romance, beautiful scents, clean sheets, two clean bodies, candle light and soft music (think classical like Ravel's Bolero). Music can change a lovemaking session from one of dull and hum drum to a life-changing experience that could set her world on fire. Which would you prefer? For a woman, the focus is not on the genitals specifically. We need an all over mind, body, and spiritual experience. When all these come together sex becomes one of bliss transcending regular physical sex.

Most women cannot focus on sex when there are dishes in the sink, the kids are crying and you haven't apologized for being late for dinner. We absolutely don't want to have sex with you if you have been rude, disrespectful, or abusive. If you have just ruined our birthday, ignored a question, or refused to talk about something, don't try to get us horny in bed. Most women don't compartmentalize, like men do. For us, its the conversation this morning, the fact that you forgot to pick up milk on the way home, and left your dishes on the kitchen table after dinner that contributes to our mood at night. Women are much more motivated and turned on by their brains than men. Our emotions play a huge role in whether we will allow ourselves to be turned on by your cute little move in bed or want to knee you in the groin.

Fantasy, role playing, reading erotica will get us there much faster than a man pushing our heads into their crotch expecting us to be grateful to give you head. Trying to thrust an erect penis into a dry vagina expecting sex to be great doesn't cut it either. We need time, attention, and long lasting pleasure. We need more than two minutes to get there. Most of us need twenty minutes to get warmed up to the idea and another twenty minutes to get turned on enough to have sex! The rule of thumb in bed for great sex is, "women come first!" Actually, I prefer, "Women come first, last and always!" The editor I fired didn't like this either. I am really glad I fired his ass!

The average woman requires the ten minute rule. My friend Ray Masten has written a great little e-book to help men understand the needs of a woman, because he does. He has figured out that an average woman needs forty minutes of stimulation and not just finger banging the vagina either. Although this chapter is about the female orgasm, I realize that both men and women will read this. It is so much more important that you men understand a woman's needs. Our cellular memory contains the DNA of our ancestors who have been suppressed, repressed, and put down. We need you to understand our needs, desires and what turns us on as well as off. We don't want to bruise your tender egos by telling you what to do, we expect you to know. Which is probably not fair to you, but I am writing this book. You can write your own with your male perspective when you have time.

Yes, it isn't fair that women don't come with a playbook. However, our children don't arrive with one either. Getting to know what a woman wants or needs has been a play as you go game, thus far. When you think about it, you have gotten off fairly easily till now. Now it's time to turn up the heat in the sheets.

This should be an interesting exercise for men to go through. Think back to when you began having sex. How often have you had sex on average over the course of your lifetime? How many of those times did you have an orgasm? Using the lowest percentage of women that are non-orgasmic as the 26% who fake it every time (because they don't orgasm—yet 40% of women have difficulties). Let's just say for the purposes of this experiment that Fred began having sex with a partner at the age of sixteen. Boys in their teens may have sex several times a day, many times a week. There may be periods when men go for months or even years without sex. There may also be periods where Fred was celibate, or only had sex a couple times a month, or less. Taking into account illness, dry spells, and a bitchy controlling wife, we will err on the low side for Fred. By the age of fifty with Fred having only one orgasm a week (which we know is probably a gross understatement) had 1,768 orgasms while his female partner(s) had fewer than 459.

These numbers are not even close to being accurate. I used the above formula to give both men and women an idea of how great the chasm is between us. For me personally, however, I know I have not experienced anywhere close to that number of orgasms, which is the reason I am writing this book. I have tons of skills and talents, but I am not great at math. I asked a man to do the figuring for me. After giving me the numbers, his comment was that it was sad that a man only had 1,768 orgasms in his lifetime. He did not comment on the much lower number of orgasms a woman would experience being 1,309 less than his. Which brings me back to the subject of men focusing on their penis. They can't think of a vagina AND a penis at the same time, because their brain does not allow it. For those men who are stuck on the number of orgasms you might have had, just know that Fred was not highly motivated sexually, because he is half dead, single as well as a woman hater. Most men have more than double the number of orgasms that Fred had in our experiment. Don't worry guys, Fred isn't real. I made him up.

We know that women are more emotional, prone to anxiety, worry, mind chatter, than men. It follows suit that women would also be turned on differently than a man. The focus is less on the genitals for a woman than it is for a man. Once our partners understand this vital difference they can implement change in their lovemaking. For most women, sex is an all-over experience that begins with our mind. First you have to make love to our mind. Kindness, appreciation, consideration for us means so much. You can't ignore us for days, then expect us to be warm and fuzzy whenever you decide you want sex. It doesn't work like that. Haven't you heard the expression, "Hell hath no fury like a woman's scorn?" What that means in essence is don't piss on us, or piss us off because we will never forget it. You want some caring and kindness, you need to give it to us first. You need to be loving and romantic with us. It's just the way we are built. You stroke us, then maybe we'll think of stroking you. That is, if the dishes are done, the kids are in bed, the dogs have been walked, and our mother doesn't call.

We like to be turned on outside the bedroom to create anticipation of what is to come. A surprisingly warm kiss in the morning that is out of character from you might help. A sexy text during the day letting us know you are thinking of us. A phone call just to say, "Hello, you were on my mind." All these things change the tone of our day and build anticipation. Knowing you were thinking of us and that you took the time to call means a lot.

Women need romance, appreciation, kindness, and respect to be turned on. We also need to be warm. Keeping our socks on can help to get us there according to researchers in the Netherlands. From my own experience, when I was cold in bed, it was more difficult to stay with the program and focused on the pleasure when my teeth were chattering.

If you want to really turn her on, do the dishes and help with the kids, and you will find her much more apt to jump into the sack with you at night, willing, eager and ready.

It is when you arrive home late for dinner without an explanation and in an angry mood. Ignore us, or grumble about your terrible day and how much you don't want to be bothered with us or the kids, and then expect us to be eager to go down on you at night? You need your head examined!

The pleasure of living and the pleasure of the orgasm are identical. Extreme orgasm anxiety forms the basis of the general fear of life. —Wilhelm Reich.

11 Types of Orgasm for Women

1. **Clitoral orgasms** result in direct stimulation either from fingers or mouth and tongue. The clitoris is the most sensitive part of a woman's body. Having double the number of nerve endings a man's penis has. Gentle pressure, concentric circles, back and forth motion, as well as some friction is what causes a clitoral orgasm. Every woman is different. What works for one, might piss another off. Direct manual clitoral stimulation is the easiest way for most women to orgasm. Waves of pleasure emanate from the pelvis into the buttocks and up the spine culminating in the brain.

2. **Vaginal orgasm** is rare for most women. Usually women need clitoral stimulation to achieve an orgasm through intercourse. Takes most women twenty to forty minutes to get there. Which can be problematic because many men have difficulty lasting that long. Take breaks, breathe, change positions often to lengthen lovemaking

session.

3. **G-Spot Orgasm**. Incredibly intense. The G-spot orgasm occurs after being stimulated orally, then pelvic thrusting back to orally then pelvic thrusting - you get the picture. Amazing results, deep pleasure. The G-spot does exist in spite of what some researchers have found. It only shows up when you are stimulated or deeply aroused. The area swells. It becomes ribbed and spongy. Located on the upper wall of the vagina approximately an inch and a half to two inches inside the vagina. When a woman is aroused, this area becomes erect (it is said to be the interior or root of the clitoris.) During arousal the tissue around the urethra becomes engorged and erect. The Para-urethral and Skenes glands produce and fill with a prostatic fluid. Very much like a hard-on for women. This type of orgasm takes time to build. It feels very intense remaining in the pelvic area and spreading into the uterus and anus.

4. **Squirting G-Spot - Female Ejaculation**. This is a very intense orgasm. Sometimes accompanied with an urge to pee. Some women never achieve a squirting orgasm as it is so powerful, anything else pales by comparison. Many men shame their partners when they experience this thinking they have peed on them. This orgasm occurs when there is a deep, connected relationship between two people. A woman has to feel completely comfortable with their partner for this to occur. This orgasm will build a deep bond between you and your partner.

5. **The A-Spot Orgasm.** (The Anterior Fornix Orgasm) Achieved by a deep stimulation in side the vagina (about 7-10 cm (3-4") deep) on the front wall of the vagina, the same wall but deeper than the G-spot is

situated. It is between the bladder and the cervix. A deep and profound almost sharp electric orgasm emanates from here. Very pleasurable. This area does not become highly sensitive after an orgasm, but check to be sure. Everyone is different.

6. **The Deep Spot Orgasm.** (Posterior Fornix) Many women say this type of orgasm feels like an anal orgasm. Located at the deepest back wall of the vagina. A hand with come hither motions, with long and short strokes will bring on a very strong orgasm.

7. **The U-Spot Orgasm.** Stimulation of the erectile tissue just above and on the other side of the urethral opening. Small area, caressed gently via finger, tongue or penis tip - powerful erotic response.

8. **Breast Orgasm** occurs after being stimulated—connected with the clitoris. Some remark feeling the direct connection when nipples are stimulated. Depending on how sensitive the nipples are this can be an amazing feeling.

9. **Oral Orgasm.** For women who have a very sensitive mouth. Through kissing, licking, sucking, or performing oral sex. Orgasm begins in the lips and spreads throughout the rest of the body.

10. **Skin Orgasm.** Skin is our largest organ. Through massaging parts of the body not connected to sexual organs. Through a facial, regular massage.

11. **Mental Orgasm.** Through a movie or visual experience. Sexual behavior in public that is viewed. Could happen during auditory stimulation or visual. Experience an orgasm through thought.

Chapter Nine
13 Shades Of Purple: An Erotic Tale

"Fuck me," I whispered, giving him permission,
taking him into my flesh, a soft invitation to madness.
— Emme Rollins, *Dear Rockstar*

BEFORE DEREK LEFT FOR work, he made the bed, while Gina took her shower. After making sure the bed was the way Gina would make it, Derek placed a romantic card with a single red rose on her pillow. He had been planning a special night for a while. Gina had been working hard on a project that was finally reaching completion. It had been a while since they had been intimate because Gina's mind was so focused on work. Derek knew by now that when Gina was stressed with work, getting her mind on sex was a major miracle. He knew he had to pull a rabbit out of his hat to get Gina to unwind enough to be able to make love. Gina was a pretty intense, focused woman. She had her own business and had a lot going on.

Derek had made reservations at Gina's favorite five-star restaurant. The one they only went to on special occasions. It was expensive, but Gina loved their wine list and their food was always excellent. Gina would be gaga over a night out where she didn't have to cook and clean up afterward. Derek had even found their favorite babysitter. Now that the kids were taken care of as well, he felt he had it all covered. He had everything handled without getting Gina involved, and it wasn't even their anniversary.

Derek had gotten a raise and had not told Gina about it as yet. His bonus was big enough to cover dinner, a babysitter, and a little bracelet that Gina had been drooling over for years. Derek had learned that gifts when there was no special occasion meant so much more than the obligatory birthday, anniversary and the dreaded Valentine's Day, the so-called "holiday." Derek thought that "V" day was a total rip-off for men. A day designed just to make men go out and spend money they didn't need to spend to buy shit that the women didn't need to have! He hated Valentine's Day.

The card on Gina's pillow was clear and to the point. "Gina, I've made reservations at Vinny's. You are invited to wear something sexy and leave your panties at home. I'll be home at 7:00 to get you. P.S. I've taken care of getting a babysitter too. Love, always, Derek" Derek felt a little hokey writing the note. He was not very good at the romance thing. But Gina always responded favorably because he tried. He always got and "E" for effort. Gina would be pleased. That was all he wanted.

Dinner was amazing. They both enjoyed a glass of wine. Gina had two. Derek needed to keep cool to drive home. He could always have another glass or maybe a little green when he got home. Gina liked a little sometimes too. It always made her relax more, then helped her let go so she could actually come. It was so much better when they both had a really good time. That was how he liked it and wished it was that way all the time.

Derek took the baby sitter home and rushed back to find Gina already under the covers, damn! He had wanted to undress her. Being able to unbutton each other's clothes always got them both turned on. There was something about undressing each other... His mind trailed off. He was getting hard just thinking about undressing Gina. He needed to quit it.

As Derek appeared back in the bedroom after brushing his teeth he pulled off his pants and was just turning around in his boxers when Gina got a glimpse of his profile. Gina's face was lit up like a Christmas tree. She laughed then threw a pillow at his erect penis. "My work here is done!" She laughed. "Did I miss something? Was that for the babysitter?" Derek did not think that was at all funny. "Say what?" Gina leaned over and pulled Derek's boxers off and began to suck his hard penis into her mouth. Derek had not even made it into bed yet and he was ready to come. As much as he wanted to just let it all loose in her soft, wet mouth, he didn't. "Damn girl!" Derek said shakily, "You're gonna make me come!" "Gina, this is your night. I get to pleasure YOU Baby!"

She threw off the covers to expose a lacey camisole top, with a panty all in dark burgundy. It revealed all her beautiful curvy breasts and her naked brown skin shone through the lace. Her hard dark brown nipples were peaking through the burgundy lace. Derek slid to the edge of the bed pulling Gina to him. She shuddered when his member grazed her soft thigh and bounced across her pubic hair. She inadvertently thrust her pelvis toward him. It was all Derek could do to not just rip off her panties and hit her like a jackhammer. He sighed and pushed Gina down gently. He kissed her mouth, a thousand different ways. He nibbled at her lower lip and pulled her lip into his mouth. She gasped and breathed Derek in. Derek kissed the right side of Gina's neck and cupped her left breast with his left hand. He was adept enough to be able to twist her nipple and continue kissing her neck, alternating between kissing and biting, just a little. Gina was not into S&M, so Derek was careful to walk the fine line between titillating and pain. He grabbed the edge of her nipple between his teeth and tugged backward towards him. Gina moaned and jerked involuntarily. "MMM baby, you smell so good!" Gina smiled through hooded lids. She was getting so turned on she couldn't stand it.

Gina was already writhing and telling Derek to plunge inside her. Derek knew it would be game over and Gina wouldn't come if he listened to her. Gina got him so hot so quickly he came almost as soon as he was inside her. He had to hold back so that Gina would get hers tonight. He breathed in deeply through his nose to slow down his mounting excitement. He moved down to Gina's vulva and breathed through the fabric of her panties. He barely grazed his mouth across her pubic bone down onto her little clitoris. It was standing at attention. In the next breath Derek breathed in swiftly and in one fast tug ripped off Gina's panties. Gina gasped, "Those were brand new!" "I'll buy you another pair!" Derek felt it was worth the cost. Although Gina was vaguely concerned about the cost, she was so turned on by his manliness and strength; she reached up to his ripped belly playing with his 6-pack. God he's so beautiful, she thought. What a beautiful cock!

Derek whispered in Gina's ear, "Turn over baby." She turned her head slightly as if to ask where are you going? Derek began to massage her calves and legs as she realized he just wanted to massage her. She loved getting a massage. Derek massaged each leg moving up to her knees and then massaged her thighs. He so wanted to shove a finger up inside her wet pussy, but restrained himself. He had heard that women prefer if men avoid the vagina until the last possible minute, it builds excitement. Women love that shit he thought. He remembered that it makes women feel more than just a gaping hole for men to shove their dicks into. She turned onto her stomach and as she did Derek's hand grazed her clitoris, she shivered a little and made a squealing sound, laughing. He grabbed her buttocks in each of his big hands and squeezed all around, needing the muscles, squeezing and releasing. He noticed that each time he grabbed Gina's ass she moaned and thrust her pelvis backward towards him. Derek had a sneaky suspicion that her ass and clitoris were somehow connected. One seemed to spur the other on. He began to kiss her ass cheek while he continued to squeeze the other. "Oh baby!" were Derek's muffled words. Derek began to forget himself for a minute and had to remember who this was for. He took his time massaging every inch of her back and neck being careful to be fair to both her right and left side. Then he turned his attention back to her thighs again. He massaged her feet carefully, then her hands, even her ears. Derek knew that huge amounts of tension were stored in the ears. He wanted to be sure Gina was relaxed. He wanted Gina to really enjoy tonight. This was for HER. He continued containing his impulse to plough into her, all the way up to Gina's shoulders and neck and then asked her to turn back over.

Derek looked down at Gina laying on the bed all glossy and aroused. "God you are beautiful!" Gina smiled. She loved to be told she was beautiful. Derek had no idea why he didn't do it more often. He could see how good she felt when she saw he meant it. He leaned over bringing his nose to Gina's and holding it there, they were so close just breathing each other in. Looking into each other's eyes was intense, his penis throbbed, dripping pre-come onto her upper belly. Derek brushed his lips across Gina's cheek and then kissed Gina on the mouth, slightly flicking his tongue into her waiting mouth. Gina didn't like a sloppy wet tongue. Derek was careful to control his kisses and keep Gina with him. He continued to make eye contact with Gina, which intensified their experience. His hand moved to gently squeeze Gina's left nipple and he lowered himself onto one elbow so he could suck and tongue Gina's lonely right breast. He bit the end of the nipple slightly. He wanted to really get into Gina right now. Again, he breathed deeply slowing down his excitement. Derek moved his leg between Gina's, rubbing her clitoris with his knee. That was different he thought, he couldn't quite reach her. She seemed to like it. She was writhing up against his leg like there was no tomorrow. Gina groaned. Derek moved down so he could use his tongue on Gina's vulva and clitoris. She was definitely wet. No olive oil needed tonight! Gina opened her legs to welcome Derek's soft wet mouth. He moved down into her vulva moving his face back and forth across her mound. He began to alternately lick the shaft of Gina's clitoris and suck it into his mouth. He tongued her vaginal opening with a rapid motion. He had gotten really good at this fast movement. He also learned that he had to vary his moves. Gina could go ape-shit over his tongue flicking her clitoris one night and hate it the next. He had to keep up and not take it personally. He knew that she liked different techniques at different times of the month. She was really amazing. Derek couldn't stand it any longer.

Gina's body flushed with excitement, her eyes dilated as she licked her lips distractedly. There was no question she was aroused, her pleasure building. Gina's breasts swelled, her nipples erect. With one finger slightly inside her moist vaginal opening, and Derek's mouth alternately licking, then sucking her clitoris. The other hand had pulled her pubic mound back slightly towards her navel causing more tension on her clitoris. "Ooh" she moaned. It felt so wonderful. She squeezed her buttocks together, while contracting her pelvic floor muscles rhythmically. Moving her hips, while continuing to contract her internal pelvic floor muscles almost made her come before she was ready. She began to moan louder which allowed her to breathe more deeply. This breath filled her lungs, which expanded an amazing feeling down into her pelvis. Gina relaxed into the pleasure. She surrendered, squeezing her own nipples tightly as her vagina contracted deeply with the squeeze.

Gina's body was undulating in rhythmic movements. Her pelvis rising and falling with her breath. In one hand, Gina grasped at the sheets. She thrashed her head back and forth, moaning. She squeezed her knees together, as the rush of beautiful energy left her anus pulsing her vagina with contractions, rising up her spinal column. Euphoria surged throughout her entire body culminating in the frontal lobe of her brain. With a smile, her body jerked involuntarily as she attempted to speak. "Ooh," was all she could utter. Her body tensed completely, then was as limp as a wilted Lily on a hot day in Georgia. She had finally done it! Her first orgasm through oral sex! It was exquisite, like nothing she had ever experienced before. Her shit-eating grin spoke volumes. Another wave of vaginal contractions surged through her body as he tried to stroke her thigh. Derek's touch was too much, it sent her uterus into spasms again. Her sensitivity heightened to the point that his touch was almost painful. Derek got the message, he lifted his hand from her thigh.

She smiled again. Her body felt more elated than she had ever experienced. "Oh my God!" she thought, she had been missing out on so much. No wonder guys wanted to have sex all the time. The only way she had been able to reach that top of the mountain was with a vibrator. This was the first time in years she had ever had a full orgasm. And without any extra help! It was about freaking time! Her girlfriend's advice about using a fantasy was what got her over the edge this time. She never realized how important it was to have her head in the game. She needed to be mentally stimulated to get there. She kept breathing and relaxing rather than becoming tense through out. The extra finger inside her vagina while having her clitoris sucked and licked made all the difference. She couldn't hold it back any longer. The other thought that crashed through Gina's foggy brain was Derek's patience. All the massaging, the nipple squeezing, the kissing, it was amazing! What a keeper! She thought back over the day's events and smiled.

Gina began to turn toward Derek, only for him to gently push back down on the bed. With a smile Derek opened the bedside drawer. Her little two-headed pink rabbit vibrator was presented to Gina. She nodded her head smiling and closed her eyes. Derek turned the vibrator on as the familiar hum permeated the room Gina was ooh-ing again in minutes, as Derek began to stimulate her with the vibrator. Within minutes Gina was experiencing wave after wave of sequential orgasms just minutes apart. Having both her clitoris and vagina stimulated at the same time, was like heaven. She began to breathe more evenly. She had a bit of a break in the action, before a bigger and more distinct orgasm began to build. This orgasm was bigger than the first of the night, which sent a huge surge of energy through her spine. It exploded in her anus, buttocks, and deep in her vaginal cavity. Gina had heard about the different types of orgasms, but had always stopped when she had one. She had never pushed beyond the first tier to get to the land of multiple orgasms. She might never come back! This was so amazing; she didn't have words to describe the magnificent feeling of tremendous pleasure that was pulsing throughout her entire body.

Derek put the vibrator on the nightstand, and then rolled over onto his back. He urged Gina to get on top. Gina surprised him by turning around so that her back was facing Derek. She lowered herself onto his penis and leaned forward. As she leaned forward taking her weight onto her hands, Derek was able to watch his penis penetrating Gina. Gina squeezed her pelvic floor muscles sequentially. Riding and squeezing Derek's cock inside of her was too much for Derek. He squirted, attempting to get the words out, "I'm coming!" Gina smiled. She already could feel Derek's member swell with a rush or energy. He done good! "Oh my God Derek, that was freaking amazing! Let's do it again!" Derek couldn't see her face, but wondered, was she really serious? She turned around smiling. "Baby YOU the KING!" Gina dismounted, while Derek pulled her to him. Gina fell asleep in Derek's arms spooning, just the way she liked it.

Gina's experience is quite normal for 40% of women. Orgasm for women is not just an in-out procedure of a thrusting penis or tongue in the vagina. As a matter of fact, most women do not come through vaginal sex alone. Most women enjoy their clitoris and other body parts to be stimulated or orgasm does not happen. As a matter of fact, as wonderful as vaginal sex is - most women prefer pleasure to be a slow build. They usually like their partner exploring her mouth, neck, breasts, nipples buttocks and inner thighs before they begin to probe or suck anything near the vulva.

If you are a man wanting to be a better lover, take heed. Your woman will wonder if you have had an affair. Just tell her you just read Jennifer's O book.

For heterosexual women, we grapple with the expectations of men. For most men, if you rub it, kind of like Aladdin's lamp it will eventually explode. Women aren't like that. Men expect women to be just like they are. Stimulate the one "hot spot" and voila! Orgasm. For most women, we need a variety of kissing, touching, massage, licking, tonguing, and fingers probing. A woman's clitoris is like the female version of a penis. It gets erect and hard with stimulation. It is gloriously gifted with so many nerve endings—just stroking it can send shivers down a woman's spine! The key is to find the best places to stroke, lick, or suck. This is a question of ATT, not the phone company. A, ask. T, touch, T, tenderly. Until we are well lubricated our skin might pull or tear. Use a natural lube like coconut oil or olive oil to eliminate ripping or tearing the vulva or perineum (area between the vagina and anus).

Our clitoris has 8,000 nerve endings to a man's measly 4,000 nerve ending penis. I say it this way, because for centuries men have felt that they had the best toy, and that their penis was indestructible and amazing. I am here to tell you that our clitoris beats your penis every time! The great thing about women is that we can have ten, twenty, or maybe thirty orgasms in one lovemaking session. Whether it is with a vibrator, tongue, finger, or leg. Even squeezing the legs together while making love can be enough to get some women to orgasm. Squeezing the pelvic floor muscles, and nipples could send some women into convulsions - the good kind. Some amazing women can think themselves to orgasm, but that is rare. The important thing to note is that each woman is different. Some women are very sensitive. They are able to orgasm easily. Others take years of trial and error with hours of lovemaking with a tender, attentive lover. I said, "attentive," not a tent of lovers.

Keys to Successfully Bringing Your Woman to Orgasm

1. Start with a clean body.

2. Romance her.

3. Help her out - take the pressure off her by doing the dishes or helping with chores in some way.

4. Make it all about her FIRST and foremost.

5. Don't zero in on the vulva, beat around the bush... Hahaha! Touch and stimulate other body parts first.

6. 10 minutes of kissing.

7. 10 minutes of light touch, neck nibbling and body kissing.

8. 10 minutes of massage.

9. 10 minutes of fingering and/or oral sex. Make sure she comes at least once before you have your orgasm.

10. Girls on top—for orgasm, or doggie style to catch the g-spot.

11. Cuddle, snuggle and hold her. Make her feel that you enjoy being with her for more than just the old in-out.

Best Positions for Women to Achieve Orgasm

Girls on Top: Facing away from partner straddling him. You can lean forward to get the angle necessary for clitoral stimulation or manually stimulate the clitoris with your finger or a vibrator.

Coital Alignment Technique: Missionary Position

Variation, woman underneath, man on top. His legs close together, hers are just outside his. Align your spinal column, placing your head beside your partner's. Man pulls out slightly, then moves his body to position the shaft of the penis to rub along the clitoris. The man shifts his position upward cupping her shoulders, but keeping as much pressure on her below him as possible, but still comfortable. With an ever so slightly rocking motion, she moves her pelvis away from him back towards the bed as he rocks away. It is a see-saw motion of variance of only 3 or 4 inches, or less, so that the shaft rubs along the clitoris. The penis is not completely inserted in this way, it can't be.

Spooning male behind woman on side: Insert penis and close legs. Woman squeezes legs together with a slight movement forward. Can position the hand to masturbate at the same time, either he or she.

Publishing a sophisticated men's magazine seemed to me the best possible way of fulfilling a dream I'd been nurturing ever since I was a teenager: to get laid a lot.
—Hugh Hefner

Turning on Your Man

How do you turn on a man? Stand naked in front of him. Or Touch him. Yup, it's just that simple. Remember men have all their genitals on the outside, that are constantly in motion. They are also thinking about sex every 52 seconds. There is a good chance that when you touch him it will be during the 52 second window while he just happens to be thinking about sex and there you go!

Seriously, there are probably times when he isn't already erect, thinking about sex, but my experience is that those are rare. Here are twenty-five hot ways to put a smile on his handsome face.

1.   Take your clothes off. Just stand there. Let him look at you. Breathe. Yes, stand there. Don't fidget. Let him look at you. Be proud of your body. Breathe. Allow him to take you in. You are sharing your body as a gift for him to feast his eyes on. He will probably want to eat you!

2.   Right there in the middle of wherever you are unzip his pants and take his penis into your mouth. Make sure your mouth is really wet and juicy; he will enjoy it so much more with ample moisture. Squeeze his buttocks, maybe even a little hard. Go on, you know you want to. From here, you can continue, or move to another location.

3.   Lean over a couch or chair and stand up. Have sex in a room you are not used to having sex in. A change of scenery or environment can be a huge turn on. Even the kitchen counter might be an exciting play area, although granite is cold on the hoocheycoo.

4.   Sex in the bathroom at a party is very exciting. Public places are a way of spicing up any relationship. Just don't get arrested and say, Jennifer told me to. I will deny everything!

5.   Hot tubs at night under the stars even in winter are wonderful exciting places to begin, but not make love. If you are sensitive you could end up with a bladder infection. We don't want that kind of pain.

6. Surprise your guy with a rose petal covered bed with a head to toe body massage. Let him relax and enjoy. If you feel so called, take over and jump on top of him, once you roll him over. Ride him like a cowgirl, YEEHAW! Use lots of coconut oil or water-based lube.

7. Elevator sex can be really a turn-on. Though these days even in the tallest of buildings they rise pretty fast. You know what happens when things rise too fast. They can end just as quickly!

8. The ocean can be great fun. I once made love off the coast of Bermuda in the ocean with my guy. A fantasy of mine has always been to be watched. As luck would have it a local watched us from above. It was quite the turn on. Go on, you know who you are!

9. Men love lingerie. Two-piece bra and pantie sets, teddies, lacey see-through nightgowns are all great. Buy something new for each day of the week. Surprise him every day! Sex every day might be more than you are used to, but he will thank you for it. He might even cry, "UNCLE!"

10. Dress up as a school girl in knee socks and a short kilt, like a private school girl. You will not have to do much to have him come all over your kilt.

11. Join your man out for dinner. Text him before hand to let him know you are not wearing any panties. You might not make it home after dinner!

12. Speaking of texting. Send him a photo of you dressed in something sexy. Leave him a message saying you have something special prepared for dessert tonight. The anticipation will make him want to explode on the spot!

13. Be really naughty on another occasion. Send a text of one of your body parts, then let him know that

you are warming up dinner for him.

14. Buy some champagne, make a picnic. Then take a blanket to your favorite park and dress up sexy for him. Men love it when you go through the effort of dressing just for him. Pack foods that you have to feed each other. Strawberries, pineapple, little smoky sausages—little wienies! (although not the healthiest can be sexy foods too). Bring some chocolate sauce to dip the strawberries in. Feed him. Don't let him feed himself.

15. Buy a sexy board game to surprise him on date night. Dress in one of your new sexy lingerie outfits. Make sure you do everything on the board you are supposed to. Don't cheat!

16. Plan for a date night then dress up like a playboy model. Wear a push up bra and a white blouse that is unbuttoned. Add some white stockings or maybe a garter belt. Have him watch you while you masturbate. This will give his engine a crank!

17. Surprise him in his office when he is working late, then give him a blowjob under his desk. He will have a hard time focusing on work the next time he sits at his desk.

18. If you make his lunch, pack little post-it love notes in it every day for a week. Then tell him one of your biggest fantasies on Friday in a card. Write that you want to live out this fantasy when he gets home from work.

19. Another day you make his lunch cut his sandwich into a heart-shape and give him sexy foods. If you have already had the picnic, tell him you want to make him your slave when he gets home tonight!

20. As soon as you are able to, take him into the

bathroom to bathe him. Make sure you wash all his "dirty" parts really well. Then take him out of the tub and dry him off, blindfolded. Lead him to wherever you want to make love to him. Lube his chest and balls with cocoanut oil. Rub just his front, massaging every detail, without touching his penis at all. Squeeze his nipples, both at the same time, then massage his feet and toes. Massage his thighs and knees and finally stroke his penis till he comes. Note to self: "This will not take long at all!"

21. Play Kim's game with him. Blind fold him. Tie him up to the bed or chair naked, but (leave his socks on) with silk scarves or handcuffs. Then touch his chest with an object and make him guess what it is. If he guesses wrong, punish him by making him pleasure you in some way (touch your breasts or finger you). Have 10 different textures to touch him with. Use some of your panties and stroke his balls with them. Cotton balls, feather, silk scarves, hairbrush... Get creative. Just don't hurt him too much!

22. I love blindfolds. Here is another way to tease and please your man. Tie him up, blindfold him naked with his socks on. Make a banana split with his junk. Whip cream, pineapple, ice cream (just a little as it melts), chocolate sauce, and top it off with a maraschino cherry. Then eat all of it without using your hands. You may want to take off his blindfold part way through, maybe not, the torture of not being able to watch may be enough!

23. Wash his hair topless. Take your time and allow him to touch you while you massage his scalp.

24. Massage his feet and paint his toenails. Kinky? Oh come on! He has a feminine side too you know. Pick

great colors make it fun!

25. Cook dinner naked night! Yup, naked dinner night. Make sure you don't choose something that splashes grease onto your naked skin.

That's all for now folks! Enjoy the fun. This is all meant to excite, pleasure and turn-on. It is in no way meant to harm, hurt, or embarrass either of you. Be playful and have fun with him. You will both open up to your child-like imaginations and turn on more than your bodies! You will turn on your minds too!

Chapter Ten
Dating And Sex

If I'm not interested in a woman, I'm straightforward.
Right after sex, I usually say, "I can't do this anymore.
Thanks for coming over!" —Vince Vaughn

DATING CAN BE FUN, exciting and exhilarating. It can also expand our insecurities, concerns about body image or even our fear of commitment. Men and women look at dating differently. Women like to embellish what is said, often creating fantasies about the men we date in our heads, which have absolutely no basis in fact. Although there are men who want commitment, eventually, some are only looking for a warm naked body to experience a physical release with, and nothing more. Knowing which one of these men you are dating takes skill, listening, and the removal of your rose-colored glasses.

If you are okay having sex without commitment, you have the choice to do so. Not getting caught up in the traditional dating ritual, having sex with whomever you want can be fun. You can have some great sex, with different partners. Polyamory is on the rise, as a romantic relationship involving more than two people. Not the same as cheating, as everyone knows about everyone else and agrees to it.

Hooking up, hanging out, and having indiscriminate sex with strangers can be problematic if you get emotionally involved. Knowing what you are getting into up front helps keep emotions in check. These types of affairs are not a recipe for a long-standing relationship. Intimacy is created when you get to know someone well. One-night stands do not develop deep intimacy. A physical act without an emotional connection can occur in these types of interactions. This is sexual gymnastics rather than a relationship. Usually, lying and avoidance come up in quick-connect type activities. Honesty is required for deep intimacy.

I recently dated a man that I met at a singles mixer. He was very nice and kind, and we had a few dinners out without any physical contact. I wondered right off the bat if he was disinterested, but just being nice. Neither of us wanted a relationship, but rather companionship. When his birthday came and went, he lied about his plans for that day. I called to wish him a happy birthday and he said he was having lunch with his sister. The week before he said he was having lunch with friends. You just don't lie to a psychic. We know when we are being lied to. We had no physical relationship and I wondered why someone would lie about what their plans were. I was a grown up woman. I could take it. Of course, he might have encountered other women who couldn't. My sense is that many men and women lie because it is just easier, or they think it is.

We need to keep our heads on straight, our feet on the ground and our skirts between our knees if we want commitment and a lasting relationship. Wanting a lasting love requires forethought and planning. To have a committed relationship, it is imperative to keep sex out of the equation as long as possible. For those who aren't concerned about longevity in a relationship, having sex immediately can be fun, exciting, as well as short-lived. Typically someone begins to care, show signs of neediness, jealousy, or wanting commitment. That is when he stops calling. Yes, it is usually, but not always, the woman who wants more.

Having sex too soon can lead women to trust where it is not warranted with sexual intimacy where there is no relationship. When sex happens too early, men usually feel if we would sleep with them, on a first date, we may also sleep with Tom, Dick, and Harry, just as quickly. This makes men squeamish. They want a woman they know or feel sure won't screw around on them. Someone who will allow them to dip their ink in her well is easy in their mind. Yes, even in this day and age, there remains this amazing and ridiculous double standard. Sadly this is true. I wish it weren't. It is perfectly okay for men, but women are easy slores, (my word, a combination of sluts and whores) if we give it up too soon. The addition of sex opens the door to the question of commitment and monogamy. It permanently changes the playing field. It can lead to disrespect. Women feel that they need to have sex to keep the man, while men lose respect for the women they sleep with, for having sex too soon. We need to have respect for ourselves, while keeping sex out of the equation, until we know that this person is one who is boyfriend material, rather than just someone who wants to get laid. Will he be monogamous? Can he be? Can he commit? Are you at the point in your dating to be exclusive? If these questions have not been discussed, the answer is a resounding "NO." Of course, these same questions pertain to women also. There are women out there who cannot remain faithful if they have to wear a burqa to do it.

Don't assume, because you are ready for a commitment, that he is. In today's dating world, many men are dating 4 or 5 women—because they can. Women of course, are able to do the same. Dating multiple people is fair game for anyone. The Internet makes it easy to have several people on the hook while having sex with all of them. I cannot tell you all the women who come to me with sad stories about the man they thought was exclusive with them. They found out he was in two committed relationships at the same time! The rule of thumb for the length of time to wait to be recognized as a serious partner is three months. Not three days—three months or twelve dates.

Taking time to get to know someone before jumping their bones builds friendship. When you get to know someone before you jump them, you experience the small things that can be very sweet. These things would be overlooked if you were already having sex. You might spend more time in an embrace, enjoying the moment and feeling their body against yours. Having sex too soon brings many very personal and private things into the forefront of your brain that you might not really be prepared for. Sex with an emotional connection makes sex so much more exciting. When you dive into bed together on the first date or two, there is little or no connection. Once you have sex, your body-mind imagines that you are closer than you are in reality, just from the hormone rush. Sex can make someone who is not good for us seem infinitely more interesting. When people wait longer to consummate their relationship, they have built a friendship, gotten to know each other better and the awkwardness of your first time will feel that much sweeter.

Trusting your heart is key. You have to use your own best guidance. There is a lot more that you don't know than you know. You can do all the right things, but you cannot control another person. When it feels right to you. Drunk sex, pick-up sex, are all setting you up for one-night stands. There is a risk to dating and sex. You can have your heart broken. There is no guarantee that waiting for three months that he/she will stay with you for the long haul. The truth is in matters of the heart, there are absolutely no guarantees. As a matter of fact, I can guarantee you that if you fall in love, at some point you will cry, other moments in time you will laugh and yet others you will wish your partner would just die already! All of these feelings are perfectly natural.

People can fool us. It happened to me. We can be intelligent, savvy, and have done years of personal growth and still find ourselves with someone who isn't who they say they are. The chances are better that the longer you remain celibate the better the chances of having a relationship that lasts. You have the opportunity to find out more of who they are by waiting. Once you take your clothes off together, you can't take it back. You are sleeping with all your partner's conquests. Having it all you have to risk it all. There is limited gain with no risk. Just like with investments, the more we risk the more we have to lose and gain.

Remember sex early means lack of commitment and respect long-term. Both of you need to have an understanding that this is not a serious relationship. I have seen all too frequently, though, that women have sex early and then have feelings for Mr. Wrong. They fall for someone thinking they could keep emotions and feelings in check. Let's face it, oxytocin is powerful. We can't fight hormones. Hormones make us "think" we are in love when it is just the wonderful hormone cocktail - literally.

If you want sex, but want to keep hormones out, have a tantra buddy. No kissing, no intercourse, and no oral sex. Keep and follow those rules. You can still get off, but not have the same rush or hormones that you do through vaginal, oral, and anal sex. Sure you might miss the kissing, but your heart remains intact, for the most part.

My father always used to say, why buy the cow when you can get the milk for free. It used to make me angry but he was right. If a guy is really into you, he will wait to have sex. If he is only out for sex and you don't have sex with him, you will soon figure that out when he doesn't call or pursue you. Call me old fashioned. Women typically have a harder time dating multiple people because we like one person more than the others. We can become attached, when the rules of engagement are not to. The ones that really like you will be slow to grope, or stick their tongue down your throat. If you still have your tonsils and adenoids, so much the better!

They may even hesitate to kiss you, because they respect you. Many men allow women to make the first move out of respect for you.

Having sex too soon sends the wrong message; it says you are not marriage material.

When we have sex too soon, we can have a tendency to disconnect emotionally. We often do this to protect our hearts. For those that can't disconnect, we may become attached and feel insecure and needy because we are operating in a false reality. We begin acting like there is a real relationship, when there is not one. If we become needy we may find ourselves in the cold, holding the relationship bag all alone.

The possibility for a quickie marriage exists when one person is trying to hide something. They may want to rush into tying the knot quickly. Beware the quick proposal. Secrets can be kept for a short term. It may sound romantic, or make you feel like Cinderella. Those who have grown up wishing for and wanting to be rescued may be perfect targets for a quick courtship and speedy marriage. I experienced this and found my husband was an alcoholic AND playing for the other team. Make a pact with yourself to not get married to anyone in under two years. This way you have a standard to live by to protect yourself. Keeping your wits about you, rather than being caught up in wedding plans too soon could protect you from serious damage down the road. These could be financial issues being covered up. Addictions, gambling problems, or other families are all possibilities when you jump into marriage. You don't want to borrow trouble by jumping into a marriage all too quickly. Marriages last longer when we have a long-standing dating history. Getting to know one another, with a friendship or loving connection can help us determine if they are right for us. Dating two years or more prior to marriage is recommended. Anything less and you could find yourself in divorce court within a year.

It is important to have the commitment to evolve and grow together. People change over time. Having a relationship with someone you like, enjoy being with, that makes you laugh can help to build a deep friendship that grows. Having similar interests, as well as a mind-body and spiritual connection, supporting each other in your life goals and dreams will create a foundation to build a lasting love on. When communication is heartfelt, loving and respectful the sky is the limit. Conscious sex lights the fire of passion, kindles a flame that will continue to grow as your sexual expression remains constant and loving. Sex is the glue that keeps your heart open, your chakras balanced, and opens the door to wealth, abundance and prosperity in all areas of your life.

Chapter Eleven
Front Door, Back Door, and Playground

Sex is not the answer. Sex is the question.
"Yes" is the answer. —Swami X

SOCIETY HAS PLACED A dark stamp of shame on sex. It is a wonder that anyone is doing it at all. Shame colors our childhoods from the time we are chastised for touching our "private parts" as children. When we are made to feel bad about our sexual orgasm, we create shame in our body-mind. Sex is such a glorious, fulfilling experience that lifetimes of shame for what we have done to ourselves and others needs to be forgiven. Forgiveness of ourselves is key to letting go of suffering. When we let go of past suffering in our bodies and minds we can experience not only sex, but life from a higher place of joy or bliss on a daily basis.

Our society heralds boys for having sex in their

teens, making them men, while teenage girls become skanks, whores, and sluts for the same behavior. Women historically have been suppressed and condemned for the same behavior that makes men studs. How can we have equality in the bedroom with a society that makes sex positive only for men? The fact that Viagra was created and not Piñata further illustrates this point.

Women still deal with shame for performing sex acts that men long for. Our expletives include putting down women and our body parts. My least favorite word in the entire English language is "cunt." Any word that turns a body part into a dirty word needs to be removed from our vocabulary. The fact that the words, "fuck you" can be hurtful, rather than a turn on, is also sad. We should be saying, "Okay, when and where?" Using words for sex that hurl anger at another, rather than love, is telling. Our society in the U.S. is screwed up. Sex that was created by a loving being has been turned into insult, degradation, and abuse. Changing our attitudes about women and language around body parts is paramount. Making sex sacred rather than cruel and hurtful comes from a patriarch-dominated society that degrades women for their body parts and ability to procreate. Case in point: "you son of a bitch!" or "you motherfucker!" When our voice equals the strength and power of a man's we feel more comfortable and safe. The fact that men want sex more often generally than we do creates issues within our relationships. We want to have our personal power, but find ourselves in the unenviable position of having to say no, when we are not interested in sex. When our men want sex more frequently than most women do, we are caught between a rock and a hard place, standing up for what we want and believe in, or having to constantly give in to our men's much more active libido. Comedian Whitney Cummings, has a great solution to our ever present issue of morning sex. She quietly sneaks out of bed, into the kitchen. She cuts a ripe melon in half. After warming it in the microwave, she puts a wig on it and slides it between the sheets! Certainly we can't substitute a melon for the warmth wetness of a vagina, but the idea really does make us laugh.

Shame is the lowest vibration that we can feel. It causes our bodies' emotional suffering. It is in no way positive or uplifting. Shame causes women to stop feeling pleasure. It often blocks women from self-stimulation. If we weren't meant to pleasure ourselves, our clitoris would be in the middle of our backs or some other hard-to-reach place. But it's not. Our clitoris is within easy reach. As a matter of fact it is so handy that our arms don't have to stretch to touch ourselves. We can very comfortably lie on our backs to pleasure ourselves. Yes, just like men do!

Most men feel very comfortable giving themselves pleasure. A hand job, jerking off, circle jerk, among many others names for what a man does for himself. For many men, it is the only sex they get. Remember, sex is natural, sex is good. I hear George Michael singing in my head. Sex is a natural need. If it feels good, do it. Isn't that the Nike tag line? A multibillion-dollar industry can't be wrong. So just DO IT! Just remember to use protection.

Some women are so hesitant to touch themselves that there is no such name for the act of clitoral stimulation like there is for a man's "hand job". How about a "clitoral clique?" Or "clit clamor?" For centuries, it has been men receiving all the pleasure, while women's enjoyment fell by the wayside.

This negligence does not help us or others in any way. In fact, it cripples us. We cannot live fully, or function at our highest capacity with shame in our bodies and minds. (The Sexual Healing chapter has a self-healing section to move you out of shame and suffering).

The Durex national survey of 3,000 Americans found that although using sex toys may seem counter-intuitive for men; women who used vibrators in the past 30 days reported higher levels of what is important in between the sheets. They reported across the board higher levels of arousal, lubrication, orgasm, and sexual satisfaction. Vibrators are like the magic wand of sex. They will enhance your play and raise men's confidence. Men found serious benefits. They scored higher in sexual function and increased satisfaction.

Using sex toys can change the sexual experience for both of you. Your vibrating partner will not replace you in bed; you can't cuddle with a vibrator. A vibrator can't take you out to dinner, or fix your car. Men don't have to worry about not being needed. A vibrator just makes you a hero in the pleasure department, with little effort.

Libido Stimulation

I love products that boost a men's or women's libido that are comprised of plant based materials. Tribal men and shaman have used aphrodisiacs for thousands of years. I have listed some of the better ones here.

I also recommend taking a supplement for vaginal

dryness. I have used this on occasion, and it works great for pre-menopausal and menopausal women. It is a fact of life that sometimes we get dry. Whatever you do, don't push forward without getting your lazy ass out of the sack to provide some comfort for your partner. The more giving you are, the more giving your partner will be. A little consideration goes a long way. Think about how you would like to be treated.

There are many ways you can light up your sex life. Erotica, vibrators, and oils will add a different dimension to your bedroom escapades. I have included some of the tools that I like to enjoy. Feel free to discover your own plethora of fun, with fabulous ways to increase pleasure in your life.

Breasts and Nipples

Women and men have breasts and nipples. Like everything else, some of our nipples are incredibly sensitive. We love to have them squeezed, massaged, or sucked. What works one day might be just the thing that sends us through the roof with too much sensitivity. Our cycles change the sensitivity of our bodies. Others don't like our breasts touched. Talk about it. Ask. Try it to see what happens. Watch your partner's face. Most women have very sensitive nipples. They love to have them squeezed, sucked, and fondled. A little nibbling play can greatly arouse some women, but be too much for others. Touch our whole breast, taking one breast in each hand while squeezing, gently at first. Ask if it feels good. Then squeeze both nipples, twisting them. Hard, and then harder. Some women are so sensitive that you can send them into convulsions with orgasm through the breast alone. So don't forget our breasts!

Oral Sex for Women

The key is to be confident, rather than focusing on technique; relax and know what you do will be pleasurable for your woman. Read this several times. Practice before you use it on a woman. Remember to pleasure your woman's body all over before you get down to oral sex. Target practice will only piss her off. You want to pleasure her all over using the ten-minute rule of kissing, ten minutes of massage, ten minutes of touching all over, finger-flicking, feather touch, then finally ten minutes of oral sex before penetration begins.

Many men seem to think that most women come in two minutes like they do. That is not typical. Less than 1% of the population falls into that category. Direct stimulation of the clitoris will certainly bring orgasm on faster than any other way.

Placing a pillow under a woman's hips thrusts up the pelvis in a way that exposes the clitoris. That makes oral sex easier to perform. You will find it more comfortable for you. Begin to lick the labia, or lips, flicking your tongue. You can gently insert your tongue into the vaginal opening, as well. Probing with your tongue gently at first until the area is moistened. Probe in and out with your tongue (tongue sex). Gradually move up to the clitoris, licking the shaft. The clitoris is very sensitive, watch to see her reaction to what you are up to. If you hear her moan continue, she is showing you her appreciation. The clitoris is amazingly sensitive with

8,000 nerve endings, twice as many as the penis. Lick the clitoris up and down. You can make her come by licking, then varying your speed to see what she likes. At this point you can use one or two fingers inside her vagina at the same time, as you orally stimulate her. Make sure she is wet enough inside her vagina, otherwise a little lube or saliva on your fingers might be required. Once she begins to move her hips and starts to come, don't change what you are doing. Changing a movement or tonguing action at this point could dissolve her orgasm. Keep it up until she comes.

A flat slobbery tongue in the vagina will not do much. Use some technique as aforementioned, and you will get great results.

Pull back the clitoral hood with your left hand gently. This exposes and places more tension on the clitoris. This will increase her pleasure. Begin sucking the clitoris. Draw the clitoris in between the lips, then keep up the suction. Suck up and down the shaft. This will be very arousing for her. The clitoris will increase in size as it is fully aroused. If she has become too sensitive after an orgasm, vary your stimulation. Instead, begin to stimulate inside the vagina.

If she has not come as yet, continue to suck the clitoris. It will become hard and erect. Once it is fully erect you can use a machine gun technique flicking your tongue in rapid-fire motion. This can feel amazing to her; keep it up as she will most likely come with this technique. Flex your tongue against your upper lip, using your upper lip as a springboard. The effect is an amazing feeling for a woman. Forcefully propel your tongue out of your mouth while hitting her clitoris until she comes. You might even hear, "Don't stop!" as she is beginning to come. Don't stop until she comes. Changing the motion or speed at this point could stifle the orgasm. This could be something you practice alone to build your stamina. The muscles in the tongue and chin can get quite fatigued. Telling her to "hurry up!" is not a good idea. It can take her level of arousal from a 9 to a 2 or 3 quite rapidly. Remember an orgasm for a woman is 80% mental if you appear impatient or sound like you are trying to push her to come; your efforts will work in reverse. Using a finger just inside of the vagina at the same time as you orally pleasure her will increase her pleasure to make her feel exquisite. It provides multi-layers of stimulation points, as well as different feelings.

Giving a woman an orgasm with your mouth is far more pleasurable than being digitally pleasured with a finger or hand. A woman can pleasure herself with her own fingers. Give from the heart to pleasure her with your mouth, this will be much more pleasurable. It's certainly more memorable for both of you.

To manually stimulate the clitoris with fingers you can use one or two fingers over the hood of the clitoris. Use either up and down movements or circular movements, beginning slowly, then quickening, as she gets closer to orgasm. Whatever you do, as she becomes more and more aroused, I repeat: don't stop or change positions! So, get comfortable before hand. Women can have multiple orgasms before you enter her. Once she has had several orgasms, the G-spot is easier to find. It will be swollen. Stroking the G-spot after oral sex will expand the pleasure she has just experienced by the power of fifty or more.

A woman takes longer to become aroused than a man does. Once aroused, she stays aroused longer but is capable of multi-orgasms or waves of compound orgasms. The more you do this for her, the more she will also give oral sex to you. Sex is a give-and-take, rather than give-and-give experience. One person giving oral and the other just receiving and NOT giving, is not equal. If you want to be treated like a KING in your bedroom treat your partner like a Queen. This goes for people of all sexual orientations.

Take your time. Don't be in a rush. Think of the Pointer Sister's song, "I want a slow hand." She speaks for all of us women. Well, maybe at the beginning of a lovemaking session. Then you can pick up the pace.

> Darlin', don't say a word, 'cause I already heard
> What your body's sayin' to mine
> I'm tired of fast moves, I've got a slow groove
> On my mind
> I want a man with a slow hand
> I want a lover with an easy touch
> I want somebody who will spend some time
> Not come and go in a heated rush
> I want somebody who will understand
> When it comes to love, I want a slow hand

The Vagina

PH balance of the vagina is critical. Normally, the vagina is acidic. This helps to kill bacteria quickly and effectively. There is no need to douche to clean up the vagina, although a wash with a warm face cloth after sex helps to keep you clean and free of infections for the most part. The vagina is like a self-cleaning oven. It cleans itself. There are new products on the market that are PH balanced created by Sweet Spot, which help keep you fresh and clean after sex. A wet-wipe for the vagina. Emptying the bladder right after sex, instead of going to sleep or doing so in the morning, is an important preventative for women, as well. Emptying the bladder after sex helps to prevent bladder infections, as it does not leave a warm, wet place for bacteria to grow.

Yeast infections can occur from the food we eat, too much sugar or even after oral sex. Saliva can change the PH. It is rare but does occur. Eating too much sugar or wheat can also create yeast infections. Taking a probiotic daily is healthy not only for the vagina, but also for the digestive system. Having oral sex or vaginal sex when you have a yeast infection could, in turn, cause the yeast infection to recur the next time you have sex. Your partner can give it back to you. Use discretion and take care of yeast infections right away. Get your PH back to normal with vitamin C, probiotic, with a healthy diet without sugar. See a doctor to be sure.

Shaving - Ladies' Choice

Many men request that their women shave their pubic hair. I can't say enough about this request. Teenage girls are considered ready for sex in many countries when they have public hair. The shaving of a natural occurring hair to make one look like a prepubescent teen is more than a little freaky, to me. Pubic hair is a naturally occurring phenomenon. It signifies that the woman is mature enough for sex. A shaven pussy does not. My personal feeling is that cleanliness is considerate, shaving can cause irritation and itching. Giving up something for another, when it could create subsequent issues is not good. The fact that your man wants you to look like a pre-teen, is problematic by itself. You choose what feels right for you. I just know that when a man requests something as specific as this, there is a reason for it. Have you done your research to find out if he is a pedophile? These things are a matter of public record. Dating a pedophile if you have small children is dangerous. You could be risking a lot for your children by putting your own children in harm's way.

Human Papiloma, Virus STDs, and Oral Sex

Ok, sex is fun, but STDs aren't. Using precautions to prevent STDs (sexually transmitted diseases) are important. Getting checked regularly to make sure you do not have HPV is important for your health. We have seen in the news that a famous actor recently got throat cancer from oral sex with his wife with HPV. Be responsible and get checked regularly. If you have an infection, get it cleared up right away. STDs rarely go away on their own. Be responsible; stop having sex until it is cleared up. Chlamydia (genital warts) can be passed even with a condom, as the scrotum comes in contact with the vulva.

Lesbian Sex

Women are women. Whether we are gay, straight, or lesbian is part of who we are. Saying that someone is wrong because of their sexual preference is not unconditional love and acceptance. I prefer the word acceptance versus tolerance. Tolerance means that you can barely stand something. I prefer acceptance. Accepting other's choices for their lives is allowing them to be who they are.

Many women who are lesbians also have issues reaching orgasm. Making love to the whole person, rather than just the sexual body parts is key whether you are straight or gay. I mention this because, after having several conversations with a couple of lesbian women, I have learned that education is key. Just because you are a woman does not mean you know what feels good for your particular partner. Trying different things in different orders and intensities can make all the difference. What works one day may not work for the next. Women are all different. We feel different depending on our mood. Talking about what feels good is as important for lesbians as it is for straight couples. Getting to know your own body parts and what feels good for you will help you more than anything. When you know what feels good for you, you will be better able to communicate that to your partner.

I used to think that lesbian women would have really great sex because who knows a woman's body better than another woman, right? WRONG! Lesbian women have just as many issues as straight couples do in the bedroom.

There is a great deal of awkwardness about how to

approach one another. When your communication is open outside the bedroom, you will be better able to understand your partner's needs and desires. Talking about sex before you have it can ease some of the tension. It can also be exciting. Everything that I have mentioned in this book about women pertains to lesbian women, also. Personal preferences aside, we are all still women.

Gay Sex

Sex is sex. Everyone has desires. I am not an expert on gay sex. I know that men enjoy other men. It is the way they were born, rather than a choice. To think that some people think it is a choice and that others would choose such a difficult path pains me. I find it erotic that there are so many ways to find pleasure.

Oral Sex for Men

Oral sex is an alternative or additional mode of pleasuring your partner. The wonderful thing about the mouth is that we can increase or reduce pressure, speed, and sensations quickly. We can get wildly creative at the same time. Oral sex is one of the experiences that I have to be in the mood for, both to give and receive. I don't appreciate having my head shoved into a man's crotch to force me to give him head. Forcing someone to do anything is not respectful. It is not cool!

Men love to receive oral sex. For most men, it is the

most intense sexual experience he can have because of the slippery wetness of our mouths. The types of wonderfully creative things we can do with our tongues. My style may not be yours. You can use what you like and discard the rest. What I will tell you is that your partner will really enjoy this. I have never had a complaint but rarely have to use my hand to assist. The great thing about blowjobs is that you can really suck at it. It will still be really great, because sucking is what it is all about. So have no fear and just relax. The caveat for men is that reciprocating is what "lovemaking" is all about. In case you don't know what reciprocating means, it means to give back what you receive.

Some of the reasons blow jobs feel so good are obvious. Our mouths are soft, moist, and sensitive. The skin on our lips is similar to that in the vagina and anus. Following are my best secrets for giving the best fellatio in the world to your man.

Get comfortable. Make sure you are hydrated. Hydration is always an important part of any type of sex. If you are dehydrated your vagina will be dry. If you are dehydrated your mouth can be sticky and dry, also. So always drink plenty of water. You never know when you are going to have the opportunity for great sex!

Have a glass of ice water with lots of ice, mints, and a towel nearby. Coconut oil is good if your mouth is dry; it's slippery but doesn't taste bad. I don't personally use anything but saliva, but you might want other options. You want to make sure that you have constant moisture on his penis, or the skin could chafe or become tender. We don't want a sore pecker. No, no, no! Melted chocolate is an exceptional addition as well for those who have an aversion to swallowing semen. You could even make a banana split then add some whipped cream in a spray can.

I like to begin with a clean body—mine and his. We never know where this will go once we get going, so be prepared for anything. I like to wear something lacey and sexy that barely covers the tops of my thighs. Giving him a visual turn-on will make him happy on so many levels. Men love to watch so give him a show. Make eye contact with him from time to time; he will love that. Remember we have more than 5 senses so stimulate them all!

I love the scene in *Father of the Bride* where Steve Martin gets a blowjob from his wife, while driving home from a party. They, of course, careen into another car as his wife attempts to "relieve her husband's stress." They sheepishly explain to the cops what happened.

You can perform fellatio in a car; you can perform it on a star. Although I don't recommend it; it is very exciting though. The very fact that you are driving a car brings in the element of danger as well. At the point of orgasm most guys close their eyes until their brain boinks out of orbit. If you have your head in his lap, you can't see what's going on down the road either. Better to be safer in a chair or on a bed.

As with anything in the bedroom, I prefer to dance around a little, tease, kiss, nibble his ear, bite his neck, and gently draw my fingers or even nails across his abdomen. Most men will jerk upright a little, as it tickles. No matter, it is part of the game. This is supposed to be pleasurable for both of you. Anticipation is the key to building excitement. So, make him wonder what you are going to do next, rather than doing target practice going straight for his penis and balls.

Nibble his stomach to gradually make your way down to his pelvic area. With your dominant hand, grab the shaft of his penis to hold it firmly, but don't choke his junk. With the other hand, cup his balls and stroke them from the perineum upwards. This can be very exciting. Watch for his reaction, then focus on licking. Begin at the base of his shaft (although there is very little sensitivity there,) lick upwards to the tip or glands. Swirl your tongue around the underside ever so slightly. Then open your mouth wide to take him completely in your mouth. It's like a dive down onto his whole shaft. Grab a little sip of ice water in your mouth and then go down on his penis taking him all the way in your mouth. For a change of pace grab a mint and suck on him with a mint in your mouth. The mint may be too much for some sensitive guys, but it does give a different experience. You can pop his penis out of your mouth and blow on him after minting him. It will feel phenomenal—wet, then icy cold. Then deep throat him. Taking him all the way in as far as you can. Open your throat by relaxing and slurping all at the same time. Some guys love to hear you slurp. It may not be polite at the dinner table, but in bed, slurping is not only acceptable—it is welcomed. Guys like to know that their penis is big enough to gag you, so don't be embarrassed if it does. Make eye contact, while you take his whole penis in your mouth.

At first, I felt embarrassed to make eye contact, because I had seen porn stars do it. That is exactly the reason you make eye contact, because he wants his woman to give him head like the porn stars do. It will make him feel more excited to see you look at him with his swollen member stuffed inside your mouth. He'll be thinking about that all day tomorrow.

Think of how you would draw a Popsicle inside your mouth all the way, then pull it back out again. Do the same with his penis. As you draw back a little do a little up down motion over the head of his dick. This will nearly make him come on the spot. Stop and go down on his balls. Take one ball into your mouth at a time and slurp them into your mouth. Give the same attention to his left nut now. Don't ignore his balls; they are left out so often and need some tender love and attention. Stroke them, then pinch the skin a little, and pay them some close attention.

While you are down here, you might be wondering who his hairdresser is. YOU! You can trim his pubic hair another time. That is a great place to start a lovemaking session. "Hey, c'mon over here, I'm going to give you a haircut, now drop 'em!" Trimming his pubic hair can be very exciting, as long as you don't stab him in the process.

The underside of the penis, then the head, are the most sensitive areas. You can do a shallow head bob up and down just on the tip of his penis to make him come really quickly. Or, take your time licking, up and down the shaft of his penis holding the base of the shaft in the other hand. You can guide how much of his penis you take into your mouth with your hand. Using your lips you can purse them together so that they increase the pressure as you take his penis in your mouth to slide down on the shaft.

As his pleasure builds, watch to see how close to coming he is. If he looks like he is ready to blow, back off, and stroke his thighs gently, or move up to his face. Have him eat you for a change of pace. This will allow his excitement to die down a little. You want to draw it out as long as you can to add to his excitement.

If you hold back too much, however, you might find an inverted orgasm happens where it's as if he internalizes his orgasm but does not ejaculate. An internalized orgasm is like swallowing within the penis. It is still an orgasm, even without the ejaculation.

The goal is to get him to be as close to reaching an orgasm without having him come just yet, then back off. Allow his excitement to die down a little, then get back at it. Slurp his whole penis into your mouth, then draw back and lick up to the tip. Swirl your tongue to the underside, where the penis is highly sensitive.

Think of your partner's penis like a Popsicle or lollipop. Think of how wonderful it feels to lick an ice cream cone with Jamaica Almond Fudge or maybe something without nuts, like French Vanilla. Think of all the pleasurable things that you like to lick when you are going down on your man. This will help you with any mental or emotional issues you might have that could potentially cause you to gag. The trick to a blow job is to relax your and enjoy. If you don't enjoy it but are holding back barf in your throat, don't you think he'll notice? It will make him feel badly. So get over your aversion. Use thoughts that will calm your mind down rather than focusing on your very full mouth. Know that you are giving the greatest gift your mouth can give someone. It is mind over matter. Get thoughts out of your mind that you are doing something disgusting. It isn't—it is loving and sensual. Once you think happy thoughts what does it matter if someone in your past said it was bad? It doesn't matter. If you are married, it is one of the extra things that will keep your marriage together. Getting head is one of the main reasons men step outside of their marriage. Most women stop giving head after they get married, and men know it. Change this statistic while continuing to love your man in this way, and he will be so happy you did.

Breathe through your nose. Relax. Remember to relax your throat. To be able to take in his entire penis your throat has to relax, opening completely. This could be something to work up to, after you have had a little practice. When it comes time for him to come take him all the way in so that his penis is at the back of your throat then swallow.

I hear women say on websites or in books that it doesn't matter whether you swallow your guy's semen or not. Ask a guy. Seriously. It shows disgust if you do not swallow. Let go of any feelings of disgust. Think of it this way, you are showing him how much you care. Swallowing is a sign of acceptance. Men love it when you do. They feel slightly sad when you spit. It is a sign of non-acceptance. There are ways to get beyond the gag reflex. The mind is the best place to start. Relax your throat and just swallow quickly. Holding it in your mouth, then wondering what to do with it makes matters worse. Your saliva will build up then you have more to swallow. Do it fast. Lick the end of his penis, then look at him.

I have a theory that the more oral sex you give your guy, the more oral sex you should have also. It is a wonderful reward for treating your guy like a King and lovingly accepting all of him.

Anal Sex

Anal sex has been employed as a sex act. It has been written about for thousands of years. Freud studied the role of anal sex as a form of pleasure. There is no doubt that the anus is a sensitive area, albeit also the exit point of our digestion system. However, when you look at the fact that a male penis is also the exit point for a strong stream of urine, what is the difference? Taking a shower or bath before sex makes sex sacred. Be respectful to your partner, shower, and be squeaky clean. The key is that your partner feels comfortable with the sex act. Going slowly while using lots of lubrication is key. A condom is recommended, as well.

Both sexes have sensitivity in the anal region. Men can enjoy a vibrator, fingering, or oral stimulation here. Both of you just have to feel comfortable with it. I cannot stress the importance of discussing this before trying it. Pushing something whether it is a penis or the issue of oral sex when it is not appreciated can create bad blood between you. I have witnessed one very sweet couple divorce over this issue. She said, "no" and he wouldn't take no for an answer. Agreement is a must. Trying something once, saying, "Never again, at least I tried it," is better than never even trying. Anal sex is a very personal issue. If your partner says, "No" let it go.

Anal sex is one of the "off-limits" acts like lusting after girls in school uniforms or using hand cuffs (I prefer silk ties, but you didn't ask). Tying up your partner, providing you don't hurt or harm them, is okay, but talk about it first. Get their buy-in before you perform anal. The forbidden has always been attractive to humans (remember Eve), so your Eve or Adam needs to be asked. Go slowly. Take extra time, and be gentle. Your partner may be very pleasantly surprised. There are many nerve endings in the anus, which can create quite a sensation when stimulated. Some women love anal. Some won't go there with a ten-foot pole, never mind a penis. So you have to ask then discuss this amongst yourselves.

Size, when it comes to anal does matter. In a BIG way. So if you have an anaconda for a penis, you will have to be extremely gentle. Or she might have nightmares about snakes for a long time to come. (I am just kidding about the nightmares guys). Use lots of lube. Try to use positions where your partner is more in control of the timing. Doggie style is the obvious position, but you can also use the missionary position with legs up over your shoulders. The anus has no natural lubrication like the vagina does. Lubrication, Relaxation, as well as breathing is required.

Of the men I interviewed, anal sex was one of the things they would go outside of a relationship for, if it wasn't offered within it. Not all women like it. Many women have intense fears about putting anything up the exit channel of the digestive system. Respect for your partner's choices must be given. Everyone is entitled to say, "No" if they aren't interested. Any experience that two people agree to that does not endanger either party is okay. Know what you do in the bedroom is your business. You don't have to have the entire community buy-in to what the two of you do privately. Any new experience can deepen intimacy. Talk about it. Ask each other questions. Have a safe word that tells the other person STOP! Trying it to see if it is for you is okay, too. Just feel comfortable during the experience.

What's so great about anal? It is a different experience. The anus is tight, stretchy, and feels different. The pressure is completely different. There are two bands of muscles that make up the anal sphincter. Relaxing with breathing helps to get you beyond the feelings of discomfort. Emptying the colon first makes you feel more confident. It can help to ease any concern that you may have of incontinence. The good news is that women are probably already having anal orgasms, but aren't aware they are. Anal orgasms feel different, deep, and expansive.

The anus itself is rich with sensitive nerve endings. It is also connected deeply with the rising kundalini energy. Trying it once may be all you need to sell you on the different experience, even if it is just giving something special to your partner, for their sake.

Shame, embarrassment, or guilt are all caused by societal programming. Sex is private. What you and your partner agree to do is entirely up to you. The more you explore, the different and more varied your sexual experience will be.

Clean, Wrapped and Moistened

The caution here is cleanliness with ample clean lubrication. Do your best to have your partner clean on the inside as well as outside. Make sure your fingernails are trimmed for any sex play. Long nails hurt. Whatever you do, do not poke, or enter the vagina EVER after anal sex. Great care has to be to keep a bacteria laden penis away from this tender area. Even the slightest bacteria from the anus can cause a raging bladder infection. Men often don't realize how close the cookie jar is to the dumpster. Just be considerate, using then removing a condom when complete for extra care. If she is going to be daring and allow you in this very private area for her, be considerate of her. Use a condom. Practice safe sex.

I am a big fan of lubrication that does not burn, for obvious reasons: it doesn't harm or cause pain to soft, tender tissue. I also prefer natural to artificial choices. There are, however, some great products on the market. I am not going to suggest one over the other. DO NOT USE VASELINE EVER. Vaseline is a petroleum product. It contains ingredients that cause it to remain where it was placed for a while. Bacteria, lint, and lots of other unwanted items can get stuck in it. Lotions, like hand creams, are not lubricants for sexual play, as they contain perfumes and other ingredients that may burn. Go out and purchase a good natural lube. Do the right thing.

Without an empty colon, anal sex can be messy. She is not going to want to even consider ever going back to anal if an accident occurs. Guide your partner and give them time to empty the colon beforehand. Spicy foods should be avoided beforehand.

Use a condom to avoid filling your partner with semen, which could make them ill. The walls of the rectum are thin. Care must be taken. Be safe.

Toys, Oils and Sex Aids
Aphrodisiacs - Libido Boosters

Aphrodisiacs have been used to increase libido, pleasure and create deeper passion for thousands of years. Making love with a clear head with focus is key. Drunk sex leads to sloppy sex. It is not what I am referring to here.

One glass of red wine can have an aphrodisiac effect to take the edge off feelings of insecurity. One glass will help you to relax, release inhibitions, and make orgasm slightly more accessible. A glass of red wine, rather than a bottle will increase circulation. It can help you relax faster than a massage. Even married women can feel inhibited. Our body image is so important. Focus on the positive. Look at yourself in the mirror. Tell yourself you are beautiful. Believe it, you are.

I have seen very large women that are amazingly comfortable with their bodies. I have also seen women who were stunningly beautiful in every way feel insecure about how they looked. It is not our size that is the issue, but the way we feel about our bodies that matters. A positive body image comes from self-love with acceptance.

Men, the same thing goes for you. Accepting yourself as you are will speak volumes in the bedroom. Feel confident. The more comfortable you are in your body, the better sex will be. You stud you!

Herbs

Damiana has been used for hundreds of years as an aphrodisiac for both men and women.

Muira puma, from the bark of an Amazon tree is also known as a remedy for impotence and sexual function. It also helps with menstrual cramps.

Irwin Steel Libido for Women - Available on the Internet and through health food stores. This enhances libido in women to effectively work in two ways. Not only does it enhance libido, but it also increases the intensity of the orgasm.

L-Histidine supports, then enhances the female orgasm.

Women's Libido by Gaia - I have tried this one. It works well. Phyto caps.

Nature's Way Horny Goat Weed - Herbal supplement that works. I took it a long time ago with excellent results. I prefer the one above, although it is more pricey.

Irwin Naturals Steel Libido for Men - Bioperine enhances erectile function and libido at the same time. Supports the blood vessel system involved in penile erection. Uses botanicals to promote sexual energy.

As a caution, be sure to read labels to avoid any combination of the following as they will lower libido when taken: Vitex and Chasteberry or Chaste Tree. Hence the name Chaste Tree.

Foods to Enhance Libido and Sexual Function

Red-hot chilies will warm your body through capsaicin. They increase blood flow, which is a good thing for sexual function.

Asparagus increases circulation in the genitals as well as the urinary tract, which is good for increased sexual function. The 17th century herbalist, Nicolas Culpepper wrote that it "stirs up lust in a man and woman." In 19th Century France, bridegrooms were served three heaping servings of the green stuff. Among other wonderful vitamins of A, C it boosts histamine production which is necessary for orgasm.

Avocado even looks sexy. The Aztecs thought of this fruit as an aphrodisiac and even named the tree, "Ahuacuatl," which translates to "testicle tree." It was banned by priests for being too sexy. Catholic priests in Spain forbade its consumption. High in B6, folic acid, omega 3s, potassium, oleic acid, and cancer fighting goodness. High in fat, which is needed to create testosterone.

Bananas are another sexy fruit full of potassium, magnesium, B vitamins and bromelane, said to increase the male libido.

Chocolate, with a high concentration of cocoa powder, is good for the heart. It causes our brains to secrete endorphins. Chocolate contains phenylethylamine (PEA) which stimulates the same hormone. Eating chocolate is sexy. Chocolate has been used in seduction rituals. It has always been considered a valuable commodity, traded by the Aztecs, connected to the Goddess of fertility.

Oysters are loaded with zinc and omega 3s.

Casanova apparently ate 50 oysters a day, to aid in sperm production with dopamine, which relieves depression.

Salmon, Walnuts, Pumpkin Seeds, and Flax Seeds all contain massive amounts of Omega 3 fatty acids which keep sex hormone function at its peak.

Pomegranates have the power of antioxidants, which protect the lining of blood vessels, allowing more blood to flow, increasing genitalia sensitivity.

Red Wine will relax you faster than any massage. It contains reservatrol, an antioxidant which increases blood flow, boosting circulation before and during intercourse.

Watermelon contains the phytonutrient citulline, which leads to an increase in nitric oxide in your body. This wonderful surge allows blood vessels to relax. It speeds up circulation. You will be aroused in less time. Think about sunny days and eating juicy pieces of watermelon outside with the juice rolling down your chin. Sexy! This is a great sexy food to feed your partner to increase arousal before sex.

Other foods said to have a positive effect on sexual function and libido are raw eggs, vanilla, celery, goji berries, pine nuts and figs. Fruits loaded with seeds are very beneficial, boasting energy building properties.

Vibrators

Vibrators can stimulate the clitoris, vagina, or G-spot with a regularity and intensity that gets a woman to orgasm faster and with ease. The most important thing about a vibrator is if any clitoris or vagina meets one, it is orgasm at first experience. What is not to love about that? Men, you will be a hero if you show up with one. You will be adored if you try sex with one.

Most men are afraid that vibrators will take them out of the game. Not so! Most men report more confidence in the bedroom after they start using sex toys. If your woman starts having orgasms each time you have sex, she will be much more likely to want it. See the correlation here? Sexual satisfaction leads to more sex, not less. The better you are able to satisfy your woman, the happier she will be with you. It does not matter how you get her to orgasm, whether through a vibrator, fingers, penis or tongue. The point is for a woman to have an orgasm. Remember she isn't satisfied until she has had at least one orgasm, or more. Using a vibrator will get her off quickly, without you getting a cramp in your neck or jaw ache. Afterwards, you can go, have all sorts more fun. Once a woman has a clitoral orgasm, the G-spot will be swollen. You will be able to stimulate the G-spot to orgasm either with a vibrator, finger, or your penis.

If you want to stimulate the anus using a vibrator, purchase one specifically for anal activity. Never, ever, put it anywhere else. Wash it when you are done with it. Keep it separate from your other toys.

Considerations

Just think how you would feel if you did not have an orgasm for thirty years. A vibrator can add a dimension to your lovemaking that has been absent—an orgasm! It can increase pleasure for your partner, which makes you look like a master. Wouldn't you rather bring your "A" game? Open up to explore sex toys. You will not be able to imagine the new dimension that opens up to you.

Vibrators for Men

Aneros Helix - over a million sold - sales speak volumes!

Lubrication Aids

A considerate lover will plan ahead and have lubrication handy. Again, using lubrication does not mean you aren't a man, it just means you are a considerate man. Women like men who consider them. You win brownie points in the bedroom by considering your partner. How does she feel? How does he feel? Products specifically created for the vagina need to be used. Plan ahead and get the PH balanced one without the sugar, scent, or heat. Many woman are irritated by scents. If the vagina is irritated, sex either won't happen, or it could be very uncomfortable for her.

Lubrication aids fall into three main categories: water-based, silicone based, and oil based. Water-based lubes need to be reapplied often, but don't become as sticky as silicone based lubricants do. The best ones for women don't contain glycerin, parabens, or alcohol.

Water-based lubricants are effective and acceptable to use with condoms.

NOTE: My favorites, olive and coconut oil, are not good with latex condoms. They corrode a condom and make them ineffective. Do not use oil-based lubrication if you are using condoms.

Chapter Twelve
Fear and Pornography

Pornography tells lies about women. But pornography tells the truth about men. —John Stoltenberg

BELIEVE IT OR NOT, fear plays a large part in women's dryness, lack of arousal, or in overall pleasure. Generations of women have been in fear of rape, molestation, assault, and disrespect. Men are motivated by sex, while women have been in fear of men for thousands of years. Laying fears to rest is what happens in a committed, loving relationship. The fear of pregnancy is often one of the biggest issues faced by young women today. It permeates our lives from the onset of menstruation through menopause. Men rarely understand how debilitating that fear can be. Abortions are not an option as protection, yet, even with protection many of us have gotten pregnant. Pregnancy changes our lives, forever. When faced with being a single parent at an early age, abortion looks like the way. Birth control is not perfect. Using it every time makes it more successful. Even when birth control is used, pregnancy can still result. It is something I had to face as a single woman. My 18-year old daughter is the result. It is not a simple decision. The energy of it remains with you in your cells. It needs to be forgiven or cleared.

One-night stands increase fears, limiting beliefs about the self, and insecurities for some women. Pornography has done more to damage women's issues with men, than it has to enhance it. We fear we won't be sexy enough, won't perform the way the porn stars do and will disappoint you in the bedroom. We can't compete with women who have breast implants and twenty-two inch waists. We are not porn stars. The standard of beauty and sexiness of porn stars creates one real women can't possibly live up to.

Women long to be accepted, revered, and loved. Porn has ruined our marriages and is ruining society. 56% of all divorces are citing obsessive use of pornography with one party. Pornography has dehumanized women. It has caused men to view women as objects. It detaches their personalities from their bodies, for their personal gratification, rather than as people who have feelings. There is a level of brutality in porn that teaches men that it's okay to be brutal with women, or cast them aside after they have come.

Porn creates boredom with men's own wives, says Rabbi Shmuley. In an interview with Oprah, Rabbi Shumley explained that pornography portrays women as one of four degrading archetypes: "They're either a 'greedy gold-digger,' 'mindless playmate,' 'insatiable nymphomaniac,' or 'one who craves pain,'" Rabbi Shmuley says. This creates the most insidious view of women, causing men to detach and not form meaningful or romantic relationships with them.

Depression Linked to Porn

Men studied in a recent pornography survey were found to have more sick days and more depression than those who did not view porn at all. Porn creates loners, who shun social interaction, which is needed for psychological health. Humans need social interaction to survive. Remember the study about the infant children who died without human touch?

Pornography, like any other addiction, can harm all that is good in your life. It hurts children, causes teens to view women in a way nature never intended for, and creates a society that is brutal rather than loving. A Norwegian study of 400 couples found that couples who watched porn together had the most satisfying sex lives with better relationships than when only one person watched porn. There are no secrets in the Universe; people will eventually find out. If you do it, your kids will, too.

Children are having their first encounter with porn as early as age eleven. What are we creating in our world? Teens are watching porn, then having their first sexual experience using porn as a guide. Many boys are growing up without a solid role model at home. Fathers fail to teach their sons how to respect, then make love to a woman. Boys are using porn as a teaching tool. Teenage boys today view girls as objects. They take their virginity without regard for what she is giving to him, or how it changes her life. Before the boy has kissed her good-bye he is lining up the next one. There is no remorse, no conscience, no regret, no feeling. Porn is creating teens so disconnected from themselves, and others. Their self-esteem is low and depression rampant. Suicide in males between the ages of 10 and 24 is the third leading cause of death in the US.

Porn is a waste of your sexual energy that could be focused in loving ways on your spouse. Watching pornography is like gambling. The first time you try it, you find it fun, and alluring. When you go back the second time, you are hooked. It becomes an addiction. Like any addiction, it can ruin relationships and families. Pornography is based on fiction; it is not real. It is like spending your entire day in front of vampire shows on television, then expecting everyone to be a vampire in your world.

Most people have had indiscriminate sex at some point. Today, my belief is that sexual acrobatics with strangers is on the decline where relationships based on love, authenticity, trust, and honesty are on the rise. Women are becoming powerfully successful in all areas of their lives. As women become more powerful, they are more in charge of their sex lives, not in fear of being alone. Looking for someone because you are afraid of being alone is the worst reason to date or become intimate. What you will find is someone who will disrespect you, then further your misery, rather than the other way around.

The Key to Successful Relationships: Reducing Fear

Self-love is the key to feeling secure, comfortable with you; therefore, you will be in a better place to find real love. Most people search for love outside of themselves, but only find disappointment rather than real love. When you are codependent, fearful or lonely, you will find someone to match you. You will find a partner who will disrespect you or cross your boundaries because you don't have any. Instead, do the inner work to feel completely happy with yourself first, then you will find someone who lovingly accepts all of you, even your quirkiness.   When you find a partner who loves themselves unconditionally, they will be loving rather than abusive.

When you long for love, or feel empty inside, you attract another who feels just as empty. Fears, issues, and challenges will be your friend. Not the comfort, solace and protection that you desire. A person who is equally matched to you when you criticize yourself will not accept you either, because you are not accepting of yourself.

Your relationship will not be successful in the long run because it is based on lack, rather than fullness. I offer empowerment courses to empower people love and accept themselves. They can go on to attract partners who also love themselves unconditionally. When two people come into a relationship already filled to overflowing, they will be much more successful than two who come together with chasms, voids, or insecurities. A relationship needs to have a dispersant of power. Equality, rather than inequality, where both parties do not make the relationship more important than their self-worth.

Frequent Bladder Infections?

Why discuss the bladder in relation to sex? This is a simple biology lesson that everyone needs to learn. A bladder infection is a painful burning with urgency to urinate, which can follow fingering, the use of a vibrator, vaginal intercourse, or even anal intercourse. Anyone can get a bladder infection. It is often associated with anger held internally. Anger about sex with your partner can cause bladder infections, think "being pissed off."

The bladder is like a balloon that gathers liquid waste; it is a reservoir for the body. The digestive system takes care of solid waste, while the bladder is the plumber for the body. The urethra is connected to the bladder. It runs outside of the body so that urine can exit. In a man, the urethra runs the length of the penis. For a man, it can be anywhere from two to eight or more inches in length. A woman, however, was gifted with a very short urethra. Even having her legs up over her head or on a partner's shoulders with deep thrusting, can cause a bladder infection. Deep thrusting with an errant finger that grazes the anus, then is inserted into the vagina can cause a bladder infection.

From someone who has had so many bladder infections that she needed to have bladder neck surgery at the age of twenty-one, to remove the scar tissue, I am an expert on this subject. Believe me, you don't want one. The burning only gets worse left untreated. There are over-the-counter methods to alleviate the burning from a bladder infection available in local pharmacies. Most pharmacists will tell you that products such as "Azo" do not clear up the infection. Most often you need an antibiotic to clear it completely. Cranberry juice, vitamin C, and probiotics can help prevent one.

Cleanliness before sex is a given. It is respectful to come to the party freshly showered and coifed. Care must be given to assure that no fecal matter is in the colon when anal intercourse begins. If a finger ends up in the anus, it must be cleansed prior to touching any part of the female genitalia. The reason for this is that the anus, no matter how squeaky clean it appears and smells, contains microscopic bacteria that cause bladder infections.

Prevention is the key. Urination immediately following any sexual activity is one of the best things that you can do to prevent a bladder infection. The longer that the bladder sits with urine inside it, the greater the chance of a bladder infection. Bacteria naturally grow in a warm, wet environment. Emptying the bladder frequently, especially after sex, is a prophylactic measure. Avoid getting one in the first place. You don't have to experience the burning with excruciating pain. Often called honeymoon cystis by urologists, it is common with a new partner. A partner that is uncircumcised can also harbor bacteria, which can infect the urethra and cause a bladder infection. This is another reason to ensure that both of you perform a sacred showering ritual first. Or arrive respectfully clean.

I found upon closer examination of what was going on with me during these UTI bouts that underlying anger was the emotional cause. Since I had been abused as a child, blame and anger surfaced every time I had sex (unconsciously). I did not feel safe and protected, so an underlying and unconscious fear was connected with sex. Our bodies have cellular memory from each and every event that occurs in our lifetime. Traumatic events are buried in our cells until we release them. (See Chapter 8 for more about healing the cellular memory, emotional field, and physical body from molestation and rape).

For every illness there is an emotional component before it manifests in the body or energetic field. If molestation occurred in early childhood, you need to clear the issue from the cellular memory and the body before this issue will dissipate completely. This is one of the reasons I became an energy healer. I knew I could clear these issues myself, without a medical doctor or psychiatrist. I no longer get bladder infections, as the cellular memory has been cleared. I have cleared the energy of molestation from my physical body, emotional body, unconscious and cellular memory, as well. I have also forgiven everyone who ever hurt me sexually, emotionally, or physically. Healing the emotional body is paramount to having successful coupling and orgasm through sex. Each of us has the power to heal ourselves with our mind. Belief is at the core of healing.

Our minds are more powerful than computers. They remember everything. Another reason you might get a bladder infection is if you have doubts whether you should be having sex with the partner you chose. The unconscious mind is so powerful that your doubts can create illness with your thoughts alone. Rape can cause sexually transmitted diseases to occur because of the thoughts of needing punishment, being taken by force, or feelings that sex is sinful or dirty. Accepting thoughts that support you and make you feel good are in sharp contrast to self-deprecating thoughts, words or emotional responses.

Penis Size And Desirability

An online study of 25,594 heterosexual men found the following:

50% of guys aren't satisfied with their penis size

In the same study of straight women:
84% said they were satisfied with their partner's size
2% said their partner was too large
Average length was 5.6 inches erect
The average single man washes his sheets 4 x's a year
Women would rather have clean sheets than a huge penis!

Relax men, women the world over are more concerned with the entire package you offer, rather than just viewing you as a penis. I have witnessed men with smaller than average packages refer to their small size so often that they create an issue. Personality, sense of humor, physical appearance, manners, intellect, kindness, and caring, all figure higher on the list for most women. If you have a huge penis but smell, the size of your junk is not going to win a lot of votes with women. Yes, there are some that look for the large penis; however, the numbers are low. Just as some people are only concerned with what you have in the bank, the same goes for penis size in the majority of women.

Whether the penis is exceptionally large, or exceptionally small both men have issues with their size. I equate penis issues like these with that of body image in women. Most men are perfectly happy with our body, whether we are lean or round. The fact that we are naked with you makes you happy. We are the same way about your penis. The programs of negativity can be cleared energetically from the field. The thoughts have to be changed. As with any program which requires consistency, lovingly accepting yourself is the key ingredient.

Cleanliness, rather than the size of your wood, matters to more women. Do your laundry, dude! Most women would rather have an average sized penis, even if it is on the smaller side, than a man who is too large. If a man is so large that he can't have an erection inside of you, his size could be an issue. Confidence in yourself and your ability to pleasure your woman figure higher on the list of must-haves than size. Everything is relative. If you have a great penis but don't know how to bring your woman to orgasm, you are still lost. Focus instead on being a better person, more loving and considerate lover. These are the things that matter to most women.

Moral of the Story

It is more important that you are clean, considerate, respectful, loving, confident, and a caring lover than what is in your pants.

Flaccid Penises

Women get dry, men sometimes are soft. The less upset you both get the better. For men under forty, a flaccid penis is most likely a psychological issue. If you have been triggered by a past memory, or have anxiety about performance, this could get in the way of your erection. Don't focus on it, don't make it a big deal. Fatigue, stress, emotional upsets along with worry can cause this issue. Drink some water, get some rest, then have fun doing something else. The more you focus on things not working, the more things don't work. Take your focus off your soft penis. You can still have an orgasm. I have seen it happen. It is true!

Change Position, Do Something Else

Stop what you are doing. Do something else. Read erotica together, slow dance or go take a bath. Let go of the reason. The reason is not the issue. Breathe. Know it is all okay. Maybe there is a better way to spend your time with this person today. Whatever you do, don't get upset or say hurtful things or blame each other. It is no one's fault. Blame will only cause you to say things that can't be taken back. Take responsibility. It is okay, things just aren't working today. "Let's do something else."

I have experienced sex with a lack of erection on numerous occasions. Massaging the prostate can do a lot for a man to stimulate him, but he has to get out of his head about his performance issues. Men can come by having their prostate stimulated, even with a soft penis.

If this is not possible, put your clothes on and go get something to eat. Feed each other sexy fruits like strawberries, figs, pineapple, and chocolate. Oral stimulation can be enough to change up the program and get him out of his head.

Play a sex game. Massage each other. Have fun in other ways. But stop trying to push a soft penis into a vagina. It doesn't work and will only serve to frustrate you both and make you feel bad.

Prostate Stimulation

Think doctor's offices, coughing. Men get prostate exams regularly or need to. The prostate can swell with age and become cancerous. The stimulation of the prostate prevents that possibility. So think about it this way: you are doing your partner a medical service, while prolonging his life. He will probably thank you for it because it is very pleasurable (so I hear).

A clean rectum and colon makes everyone feel more comfortable. You can use a medical grade latex glove or purchase non-latex if he is allergic. If you feel daring, you can use a bare finger. Be sure to trim your nails and any hangnails. This goes for men, too, when they are manually stimulating a woman. Always use a lubricant, as the anus has no lubrication of its own. Lubricate your index finger. Gently insert it into the man's anus. He could be laying on his back with his knees up. Slowly insert the finger into the first ring of the sphincter muscle. Allow him to adjust to this feeling. Have him breathe. Gently insert your finger a little deeper till you feel a bump like that on the end of your nose. That is the prostate. It is located approximately 3 - 4 inches inside the rectum. Massage the prostate gently watching your partner to see his response. Using a Helix vibrator makes it so much easier increasing pleasure for you both. You can use the Helix vibrator during intercourse for a more intense orgasm.

Prostate stimulation during intercourse can make the orgasm more intense, last longer. It also helps to keep the prostate healthy.

There are considerations for prostate massage. If the prostate is enlarged and painful or you have bacterial prostatitis, use some colloidal silver or get an antibiotic to clear it up. Too much sex or too much sitting can also cause prostatitis. If this is the case colloidal silver or antibiotics will be of no help. Antibiotics only help when there is an infection. Massaging once the enlargement has cleared will be much more comfortable and pleasurable.

Aging with Ease

Aging is part of life. Growing older is a good thing. We have more wisdom, more time, and hopefully more happiness. I have become so much happier as I have aged. I am happy with me, my life, my children, my mother and everything around me. I don't fight everything around me anymore. I am not in a war with any of my ex-husbands. I am at peace with my past, comfortable with the present, and hopeful about my future. Living in the present is part of wisdom. We learn to recognize that life is a game. It's a joy to play it. Recognizing that some of our body parts aren't what they used to be, that our strength might not be as great as in our younger years, or that we might not be able to read without our glasses on, are some minor drawbacks. Overall, though, life itself is better.

With age come some limitations. We learn that we don't race cars anymore, and we might not dive off the high board at the swimming pool anymore, but that's okay. Living on the edge was something we did when we had something to prove. Now we don't have to prove anything. We might drive a Porsche, but we don't race it on the autobahn, we live life a little more safely. Sure, we still take risks with love, maybe even in business, but we recognize our limitations, learning to make the best of whatever they are.

Dryness is one of the issues that we face as women. There are wonderful lubrications on the market. Heck, there is even some crazy scientist who has discovered he can inject stem cells into the vagina to help make it younger! I am not sure if you want to revert to your pre-virginal state, but apparently for $1,500 a pop you can have the vagina of a twenty-two year old, if that is what you want.

I prefer to accept my body as it is. Rather than fight the laws of nature, I can still enjoy sex, lovemaking and relationships -- but not with 30-year old men. I know my limitations. That is not for me. I might look at his ass as he walks by, but I don't grab it. I admire and smile.

Dealing with our limitations in a healthy way is key. Accepting the way things are, rather than trying to swim upstream like the salmon do and fight the laws of nature, is just easier. Eating a healthy diet, getting regular exercise, with enough sleep, helps to create a healthy and youthful body is ideal. Our attitude is key to our happiness and general well being. Thinking of a life that works for us, rather than against us, works well, supporting us, in a positive and grounded way.

A penis that can't get fully erect is not a heartbreak when you accept yourself and are happy with life. There are plenty of other ways to pleasure each other as we age. Sometimes, just getting in the hot tub naked with a glass of Pinot Noir may be all the excitement we need for a glorious evening. If lovemaking results, great. If not, cuddling is fine, too.

Life is too short to fight it every inch of the way (pun intended). There are wonderful ways to share travel, adventure, or family that bring a great deal of joy. Sex as we age may still happen, but it is not the pressing need that it once was. We all need to feel loved and appreciated. We just get more creative as we near our 80s and 90s. Yes, we still feel urges. Yes, we still feel and enjoy pleasure. In some ways pleasure is that much sweeter because we are so much happier with ourselves. We find pleasure in a smile, with eye contact or a kiss, as well. Swinging from a trapeze over the bed is less important in our 70s than it was in our 30s. As Rodney Dangerfield said towards the end of his life, "I'm at the age where food has taken the place of sex in my life. In fact, I've just had a mirror put over my kitchen table."

If one is lucky, a solitary fantasy can totally transform one million realities. —Maya Angelou

Fantasy - A State of Mind

Fantasy taps into the untold depths of our imagination. It excites not only our bodies but our mind, as well. A mind without imagination cannot conceive of the limitless possibilities of the future. An active imagination gives our thoughts wings. Albert Einstein considered imagination more important than knowledge. Creation comes from the ability to imagine. Give your thoughts wings to create from the expanded place of daydreams. Give your mind an orgasm, then create your own personal fantasy.

Lovemaking, without the limitless power of imagination, is two-dimensional. Include fantasy and sex, then the entire process becomes limitless, expansive, and much more engaging.

Married couples often use fantasies to spice up their relationship. After twenty, thirty, or forty years together, there is little that comes as a surprise. Using a fantasy to ignite passion increases arousal. It keeps partners together. It can also be used to disassociate when one of the partners has had abuse in their past. Using a fantasy to go to, rather than communing and connecting during the lovemaking process, can be a way to create distance from your partner. Confusing? Use fantasies to help you ignite the fires then get them burning. At the same time, stay connected with your lover to be with them in the moment. You don't want to disassociate from your partner, instead, stay connected.

Masturbation, with a fantasy, can create arousal of the mind when there is no partner present. Fantasies are both situations that a person dreams of happening with scenarios that they would never dream of participating in. Having sex in a public place might be something that titillates the mind, but the idea of strangers seeing you naked could be beyond your ability in reality. No matter what the fantasy is, the use of one can change a sexual experience from ordinary to extraordinary. Turning on the mind first allows women to ignite the passion so that their body can be turned on. If the mind is somewhere else, you are disconnected from your body. Stimulation with arousal is happening to a robot. No one wants to make love to a robot. Connect with your mind to allow your body to be aroused. Reading these fantasies can be a stimulus, which allows you to discover which fantasy turns you on. Everyone is different, what works for one person may not work for you. Deep arousal begins then ends in the mind. Any trigger during lovemaking could shut off your arousal to cause your body to stop feeling pleasure. Stay connected in your mind. Allow your body to move you. Allow your body to warm. Next, begin to buzz with excitement.

If you still feel stuck after reading this book, perhaps you could benefit from working with a compassionate and trained sex coach—someone who has been there, also. Everyone deserves pleasure. Allow your mind to take you there. Working with a coach can help you get over any fears that may be coming up of you. There is a way. You can do it. Perhaps you need a little personal assistance from one who has healed their pain from past experiences. Letting go requires you to relax the mind to let go of judgment, criticism, and condemnation. You are beautiful. You deserve pleasure. You are worthy of love. Let go of any thoughts other than those that are loving, accepting, and nurturing.

When asked, most women would tell you that they

may fantasize, but they would never perform such acts in real life. This may be true for most fantasies, but they have a secret desire to perform some of their fantasies.

As a writer, I have an active imagination. I have fantasized about sex in public, group sex, an orgy of a circle of men and women performing oral sex and making love in one room. These are acts that I only fantasize about but don't want to participate in. The fantasy itself is the turn-on for many women, but the act of performing the fantasy does not occur to most women.

The movie Tom Cruise starred in, *Eyes Wide Shut*, had been a fantasy of mine for many years. A coven, men and women performing sex acts in front of one another wearing only capes, totally naked underneath, is titillating for some. Most people won't admit to having a secret desire to either watch others making love or be watched; however, it is a secret fantasy of most women. Voyeurism is naughty. Secretly, women love to be naughty. However, our bad girls are buried under years of social conditioning of needing to behave. Being a good girl is not near as much fun or as exciting as misbehaving while being BAD is.

Most women fantasize about having sex with two gorgeous men, who ravage her, adore her, and worship her. Making love to two men is a big taboo, which is exciting in itself. This fantasy is about power. Having one man rocking her body with pelvic thrusts, while she goes down on the other beautiful man, and changing places to make sure she is totally satisfied, is an exhilarating fantasy.

Believe it or not, women also fantasize about making love to their partner with another woman. Sharing their partner's erect penis while performing oral sex together on their aroused man is often a turn-on. Watching him pelvic thrusting into another woman makes you want him all the more. You might even perform oral sex on the other woman in your fantasy if you are daring.

Most women dream of dancing and stripping for their man. We might even envision ourselves doing a pole dance gracefully, giving you a lap dance afterwards. However, to let go and be comfortable enough to dance naked or nearly naked, takes a powerful body image. It does not matter how perfect our bodies are; it is our body image that dictates whether we would ever go through this exciting fantasy for you.

Having sex with a complete stranger is one of women's favorite fantasies. To be able to have sex with absolutely no strings attached without even knowing a man's name is incredibly daring and exciting.

Being turned over our lover's knee and spanked, while dressed in a schoolgirl ensemble, can be very exciting to many women. Men, too, enjoy this fantasy. The taboo of thinking of having sex with an underage girl can be very exciting for men, as well. Being spanked can be more than a fantasy for many women. However, before you attempt to slap, spank, or whip a woman, talk about it. Be sure she is comfortable with the act. Brutality can easily get out of hand. Most women may want to experience it once but never go back there again. The important thing is that women want to be sure they can feel safe.

It is quite common for a woman to fantasize about being dominated by you. Having a man rip open her shirt, rip her panties off at the hips (without hurting us), then using some force to throw us onto the bed while opening our legs with your knee, can be enough to get many women wet. As with the fantasies above, if you are considering acting any of these fantasies out, be sure that your partner is up for it and knows what is involved. Some women really get off having their asses spanked. It tightens the vaginal muscles and makes the clitoris tingle, I hear. This is not one of my fantasies, I had far too many spankings as a child. Strike this one off the list for me.

Women have a smug smile on their faces when they talk about dominating you. Many women get really turned on when you are begging for it. The thought of being tied up, with a silk tie, blind folded, squeezed, prodded, but not allowed to touch, unless your partner says so, sends shivers down the backs of many. Having you totally worship her and her body is a great turn-on for many women. Domination of men is very exciting because it means we are in total control. The power of this fantasy is very exciting. Just remember this is a chapter on fantasy. Many women fantasize about these things but would not dream of doing them. Talking about fantasies can be enough to turn you both on.

Exhibitionism is very exciting for many women. Fantasizing of taking their clothes off, panties in a public place while throwing them at you or having sex in a movie theatre, or even in a vehicle, can be an exciting fantasy.

If you have difficulty getting your imagination engine turned on, watch one or two of these movies. You don't have to watch porn to get turned on. Some of my favorites of all time are, *Body Heat*, *Nine-and-a-Half Weeks*, and *Against All Odds*. The later has always been a favorite of mine for hot sex. *Against All Odds*, with Rachel Ward and Jeff Bridges, was powerful because of the forbidden fruit storyline. Naked, hot sweaty sex in a cave in Mexico was raw, animalistic, and such a turn-on. Few movies have that effect on me—twenty years later, though, I still remember this one. *Nine-and a Half Weeks*, with Kim Basinger and Mickey Rourke was a very sexy movie, as well.

Using a fantasy to turn yourself on is nothing to be ashamed of. A fantasy can crank up your love life and get you motivated to have sex when you aren't interested at all. Use a fantasy during the day to warm you up so that when your guy comes home you are halfway there is a fantastic idea. Whether you are thinking of your husband or a stranger, it does not matter. What does matter is that it spices up your sex life. It can get your engine revved up. Imagination with fantasies can help you with role-playing, which can be a lot of fun, providing the neighbors don't catch you. Or maybe that could be a turn on, too. Reading erotica can give you lots of new ideas for fantasies if you can't come up with any yourself. Your imagination needs to be used. Children play with fantasies all the time. As adults, we tend to lose this part of ourselves, but it doesn't have to be that way. If a person as intelligent as Albert Einstein thought imagination was more important than knowledge, we can, as well. Bring your mind into a state of orgasm with your personal fantasy.

Erotica

Erotic novels can excite the mind, lighting the flames of desire, that may be dormant. Even while reading this book you may find yourself getting excited from the words on the page or some of the suggestions that have been provided. Sometimes, when we live alone without a partner, we shut down the sexual side of ourselves thinking it is not beneficial to get turned on. Why? It is a part of the human experience. Our sexuality is as natural as breathing. Being shut down is unnatural. It is unhealthy. For optimum health, all parts of the body need to be functioning. Strangely enough, women who have turned off their sexuality often have problems with foot pain, bunions, among a variety of other issues that stem from closing off the sexual circuitry.

Sex is as normal for a humans as breathing. Shutting it down is not operating at your highest and best. Consider self-pleasure when you live alone. Make sure to keep all systems are GO!

Chapter Thirteen
Good Girls Don't, and Bad Girls Have Way More Fun

I will always be the virgin-prostitute, the perverse angel, the two-faced sinister and saintly woman. —Anais Nin

OUR FAMILY OF ORIGIN has instilled most women and men with the "good girl syndrome." We all have these ideas of what is too naughty and what we just don't feel comfortable doing. Where problems arise is when we stop having fun because we feel that we feel something is too naughty for our filters and programming.

Filters are what our families give us. We are programmed from a young age to believe certain things. These beliefs color our world. We view everything through these filters. Sometimes the filters jade us. We are discouraged from doing things that "good girls won't do." For example, my parents raised me to believe that I had to be married to have sex. Not that I didn't have sex outside of marriage. I married earlier and more quickly because my family frowned upon sex out of wedlock. I felt guilty for sex, out of marriage.

Oral sex may be one of those things that you won't do. From someone who had to get over old programming, oral sex can be as exciting for you as the receiver. Not to mention the pleasure that you give to your partner can bring unlimited excitement to you, as well.

Asking for What You Want - The Nice Way

Pleasure is different for everyone. It can even be different from one day to the next. Telling your partner that you like what they are doing, offers encouragement, appreciation for their technique, stamina, and makes them feel good. You are filling up their self-esteem bank, which is a good thing. There is no place where a person can feel more vulnerable than when they are lying naked in bed.

If you want your partner to change something or do something different, offer praise first for what they are doing that feels good. Give them encouragement. Even if it is a YES! YES! YES! After telling them they did something well, then ask for a change in technique without bashing them.

"I love it when you squeezed my nipples yesterday. Today, however, it is too much. Could you go a little easy on my breasts, as they are feeling sensitive? Thanks, Baby." The first option is highly preferred as opposed to saying, "Damn it, you are hurting me, you idiot!" Kindness will get you far, especially in bed. Be sensitive to your partner. They are trying really hard to please you. Their ego is never more exposed than when they are knee deep, going down on you. To say, "That sucked!" could mean you never get head again. Be kind. Praise what was great and worked for you, then tell them, "Could you loosen your grip a little, thanks baby".

Talking Dirty

One of the ways you can spice up your sex life is to talk dirty to one another. You don't have to use any words you are not comfortable with. You would be surprised at how pillow talk can spice up your bedroom adventures. Even if you haven't done it before, now is as good as any to begin. You can express yourself in words, what you want to do to the other person. You can also use words to tell your partner what you want them to do to you. A well-placed whisper in an ear, "I am going to give it to you hard tonight!" can leave your partner thinking about what you said all day long. You would be surprised how exciting and different your sexual experience can be with the addition of a few words of encouragement like, "OH YA BABY! Oh I love it when you do that!" or, "Harder! Harder! Harder!" Grammar, sentence structure, and punctuation will not be graded for those concerned about how you sound. This is a time when it may be impossible to complete a sentence. For those of you with imaginations the size of a small pea, here are some suggestions to get you started on the velvet verbal pleasure road. Remember we have more senses than one. Use sight, sound, touch, scents, and taste to arouse yourself and your partner. Talking dirty or using sexy pillow talk is a way to turn on your mind and your partner's, as well. Sex is greater than a physical experience. Engaging all parts of the self is what makes sex more exciting, magical, and blissful.

Phrases to begin talking dirty:

Oh I love that
Do that again
Right there baby
Don't stop
YES! YES! YES!
Do it harder!
Squeeze it!
Touch me there
Kiss me here
"F" ME Right Now!
Harder, harder!
Faster!
This feels so good!
Feels so good (complete sentences are not necessary)
Do it to me now!
Give it to me!
Bite me baby!
Oh yah baby, right there!
Don't stop!
Uh Huh!

Chapter Fourteen
If Sex is Not a Priority, It Needs to Be

There are only three things women need in life:
food, water, and compliments. —Chris Rock

IF YOU ARE MARRIED and not having sex with your husband or wife, you need to be. Marriage without sex is not marriage. If two people are married, living together and not having sex you are roommates. You are actually not growing—instead you are waiting to die. Sex is an intricate part of marriage. It is the glue that holds a marriage together. Sex is what increases intimacy and opens the door to deep conversations and connectedness.

When couples are not having sex little eruptions of unrest and arguments occur regularly. Complaints, criticism, and negativity permeate your life. Instead of having sex to bring you back to center and closer to one another, you continue to remain disconnected and separate entities. Resentment builds resulting in anger and blame. Men will stray. Affairs take you further away from love and move you to living separate lives under one roof. Neither one of you can be happy with this situation. There is nothing good that comes out of a sexless marriage.

I understand post menopausal feelings. However, your husband still has sexual desire. Not having sex means you are giving your blessing for him to have an affair. Even though you might secretly wish he would - you don't really mean it. At the first chance you would divorce his ass and sue him for everything he is worth (which divided might not be as much as you would like). You are turning your back on your partner and your love. Remember what and whom you fell in love with. Remember how cute you thought they were?

A sexless marriage is tortuous and passive aggressive on the part of the one saying, "no." Try to put yourself in your partner's place. Can you love them enough to move towards them instead of waiting for them to make the first move? I remember having self-righteous anger. Saying no and lying in bed sleepless wondering why I was being so freaking stubborn. The after-sex cuddling is so awesome. I missed it. I was hurting myself and didn't even realize it.

There is a way to break back into sex, gradually. Our libido lags when we stop having sex. Tissues become tender and sensitive when we have sex only once a month or less. Regular sex will increase the release of hormones, help you look and feel younger and help you feel happier. So what is the reason you stopped having sex?

Are you angry, upset or resentful with your spouse? If you are why are you not discussing the issues? Is the reason still present? Can you forgive each other, even if you feel you are the aggrieved party? Force is met with equal force. Instead of blaming the other person, can you be willing to let go of being right? Being right forces the other party to be wrong. When you focus on being right, nobody wins and everyone looses.

Forgiveness

Forgiveness is not for the other person, but for you. Letting go of old anger and hurts is beneficial for your health and relationship. Staying angry and upset is not beneficial for anyone and can even cause illness and disease. You fell in love with each other for a reason. Isn't it time you let it go? Are you using a past issue to disconnect from your husband or wife? Most of us make stories up in our heads that have little to do with who this person really is. When you are unforgiving you are saying you will throw the baby out with the bathwater, rather than accept your partner for who they are and forgive them.

By forgiving your partner you are saying that your relationship is stronger than any misstep that has taken place. Forgiveness allows you to weather the tough times. This is when a relationship really begins to deepen and become great. It is the best way to build a better relationship. Forgiveness means it is done and you don't have to bring it up ever again. Continuing to bring up an issue means you have not really forgiven them.

Sometimes we get to a place of impasse. It is like a

Mexican standoff. Neither party wants to give in or say they are sorry. This is not getting you anywhere. In fact, both of your little children have shown up. Adults are no where in sight. If you are going to be in touch with your inner children, why don't you kiss and make up. That is what a child would do. They do not hold a grudge.

Falling Out of Love

You might even feel that you don't love your spouse any longer. Love and hate reside along the same continuum. They are just opposite ends of the spectrum. Most of us feel hatred at some point towards our spouses and wish they would just die. Believe me I understand. However, how would you feel if they did die? Once someone is gone, it is too late to have regrets and wish you had done something different.

I miss my ex-husband. There is no way I can get him back. Yes, he was a son of an abusive, controlling man. Yes he hurt me. Yet the last two years we had come to an understanding and moved beyond the finger pointing and blame. We had come to accept each other as we were. I am at a point in my life where I have forgiven all those past transgressions, and just wish he was still here. He knew me better than anyone. He was an amazing person to bounce ideas off of. I only hope that I can spur you on to think differently about your relationship and get out of your ego long enough to love yourself and your partner enough to move towards them.

Authenticity is the cornerstone of intimacy. Being completely transparent and true to yourself transforms sex from sexual gymnastics into something really profound and spiritually connected.

Anger and Attachment

What is anger? It is an attachment to something. Sometimes we get angry if we can't make someone do something. Have you made a story up in your head about an issue? Are you being authentic? Perhaps there is an issue within you that has absolutely nothing to do with what the real issue is. Are you focusing on what other people are doing rather than focusing on yourself? If it doesn't belong to you, let it go. It makes your day so much easier, when you do what you are supposed to do rather than focusing on what someone else is doing. Hanging onto past hurts and resentment will cause you to live in the past and continue to feel vindicated for your anger.

I have an easy way to forgive. You don't even have to discuss the situation with the person in question to have it work. Kahuna healers have been using this technique for hundreds of years to heal physical hurts and suffering. Think about the person and situation and then repeat this prayer until you feel complete.

I am sorry
Please forgive me
I love you
Thank you.

Now that you have done the exercise above, begin to open up to the idea of having sex again. Getting a pendulum to begin to swing from a stopped position requires quite a lot of impetus. Your impetus is keeping your marriage alive. You don't want a divorce. Wouldn't you rather have a marriage that is loving and supportive than one that is dead? You will both be so much happier when you begin to have intimate relations again. Your husband will feel loved and accepted and you will feel closer to him. Husbands will be more apt to talk about issues and feel closer to you when you are giving yourself sexually to him. Deep intimate discussions stop taking place when sex stops. Men need sexual activity to feel intimate. Women need intimacy to have sex. Getting over the hump takes a little time.

Sometimes we stop having sex because we have had children and life gets crazy. Sometimes we stop having sex because one or the other of a partnership doesn't feel sexual any longer.

A gentle approach is required after a long period of abstinence. Getting naked with one another without actually having sex is the first step. After years of non-sexual relationship, it is like starting all over. Begin by just touching each other without the end result actually being sex. Start touching each other's hands or feet. This experience will not culminate in sexual touching. No touching of breasts, or genitals. This experience will just be to feel each other's touch. Sensual stroking and touch is the goal of your first encounter with one another.

Attending a Tantric yoga class or Tantra puja is a great way of experiencing each other differently. It will move you out of your comfort zone, with your clothes on in a safe place. Having a coach help you through the first few weeks of re-discovery can be beneficial as well. Private coaching is what I do to help partners or spouses pick up the pieces and get beyond a dying relationship. It is possible. I have faith in you.

Jonathan Robinson has a great book out that I recommend to help you communicate with one another. *Communication Miracles for Couples: Easy and Effective Tools to Create More Love and Less Conflict.*

He cites acknowledgement, appreciation, and acceptance as the key ingredients for clear and open communication.

Chapter Fifteen
Orgasm for Life

HOW CAN WE LIVE in a state of orgasmic BLISS?

An orgasm is about experiencing pleasure. We can experience pleasure all over our bodies. Pleasure can be found in all areas of our lives, not just in the bedroom. Whether it is enjoying a kiss and a cup of coffee with our mate in the morning, or making love in the afternoon, pleasure can be found in a multitude of situations. Bliss can be found anywhere you can experience pleasure. Bliss can be found holding your newborn infant.

For me, I find being in nature orgasmic. Every time I drive into Hollywood and see palm trees and realize I am in California, I feel ecstatic to be alive in this time and here in this beautiful place. I feel bliss every day.

I see the streets that have songs named after them, I

feel bliss. I feel bliss every time I walk on a beach or swim in the ocean. I feel bliss when I visit with my children, my brothers, and walk my dogs. I feel bliss when I talk to my mother, on the phone (that is an amazing thing to me).

Bliss is everywhere you find it. When we look for it, we see and experience bliss everywhere. A visit with a dear friend, reading a letter from a client from across the world, that you helped find a partner and is now married and expecting their first child, this is all BLISS!

It could be coaching someone and helping them find their soul mate, which I love to do. It could be enjoying self-pleasure and experiencing an orgasm all by yourself. It is making love with your Beloved and connecting on a deep soul level—experiencing profound BLISS together.

I find Bliss everywhere every day.

Being alone and quietly meditating brings me bliss. Eating a favorite spinach omelet I just cooked or a fabulous green salad brings me bliss. When we breathe deeply and feel so wonderfully alive—that is BLISS, also.

Knowing that you are authentic, holding nothing back, and expressing yourself fully is amazing BLISS!

We all want joy and pleasure. Being able to discuss our desires and needs with our partner opens us up to the infinite possibilities of our relationships. Knowing that you are fully present with someone rather than disconnecting, is bliss. We have a tendency to multi-task instead of focusing on who is with us here and now. Being fully present with someone else, not only brings you bliss, but it also brings them BLISS.

Orgasm for Life is about living fully, present in every breath—being with your partner fully, listening, connecting, and expanding your lovemaking to include different experiences and maybe to trying some new toys. Orgasm for Life is being open to new experiences and trying new things. Orgasm for Life is about listening to what your partner wants without condemning them for their desires. It is about LOVE.

Love is what we all want. It is what makes us human. We all have a biological need to be loved. Orgasm for Life is about setting aside your fears and doing it anyway. It is about living fully. It is about throwing our arms back like a pair of wings and expanding our lungs with a huge intake of breath, opening up our hearts to give and receive love.

Bliss can be a breath. Bliss can be a beautiful sunset. Bliss and joy is our experience when we are comfortable with ourselves. The more comfortable with ourselves we are, the more joy and enthusiasm for each experience unfolds into our life.

Being open to receive pleasure from another, means you know you deserve it. You are worthy of love, pleasure, and all manner of BLISS.

Orgasms are about letting go. When we surrender all control, surrender all fear we are no longer gripping the window ledge of life. We are in a complete state of trust. Trust is what builds a deep connection, intimate experiences and wondrous bliss. Remember that hanging on for dear life blocks living in BLISS. I know you can do it. I let go, I surrendered. If I can do it, anyone can!

The more accepting, kinder and loving we are of ourselves, the happier we are with life. Little things thrill us because we are not focused on the negative that everyone else focuses on. Instead, we focus on the miracle of life, how wonderful it is, and how great things are when they show up because that is what we expect.

When you are a glass-half-full kind of person, everything shines. We see the good in others, their gifts, and what they have to teach us. It is not that we see ourselves as better than another; on the contrary, we see ourselves as equals. Everyone has something to contribute. We learn from all that we come in contact with, as they are our teacher. Everyone has gifts to share. We are open to receive them.

The more pleasure we give to our partners the better we feel. Perhaps the joy in an orgasm is all about pleasuring the other person. The more we help the other person get there and enjoy pleasure along the way, the better we feel about giving. We get turned on by giving pleasure to our lover. Maybe the ultimate orgasm is the one that we give to our partner.

Being honest means being transparent. Deep and profound intimacy is the result of complete transparency. You don't have to remember what you told whom. You can relax, letting go instead. The more open our communication is about everything, including sex, our desires and dreams the better our relationship will be.

If you can't tell your partner what you want and need in the bedroom, you cannot be intimate with them. Discussing sexuality is part of intimacy. Intimacy is not just about having sex, it is also about our connection with another. Mind-body-spirit connection is what creates a dynamic flowing relationship. What are you afraid of? Are you afraid of letting them in all the way?

Lovemaking does not have to be confined to the bedroom, segmented off from life. Lovemaking takes place in our day-to-day life. Being kind to your partner outside the bedroom. A simple, loving look over the dinner table, a conference table, or at a Starbucks. Rather than confining sex to when we take our clothes off, we are actually making love to our partners all day long. We don't traditionally look at our relationships that way, but we need to. If we aren't loving them, what are we doing?

Our goal is to be the master of our love life. To be there for our partner mentally, emotionally, and spiritually. To know your partner, their body, expression, and the different tones in their voice is mastering our love life. It is also about getting to know ourselves. Without self-knowledge we cannot possibly communicate our needs or desires to another.

Tony Robbins is known, among other things, for asking the question, "What can I say to you so that you know I truly love you?" Tony says that if your relationship isn't growing, it's dying. I agree with Tony. We have to be dynamic within our relationships. They are living, breathing entities, rather than static. What is it you need from your partner that lets them know you truly love them. What is it they need to say to you that lets you know they truly love you?

What could you do that would let that other person know that you completely love them? Ninety-five percent of a good relationship is having the right partner. Maybe you already have the right partner, but the love has waned. It would be easy to run away and blame the other person, but what about re-selecting instead? Who are you going to be? Focus on being the best person you can be and bring the best out in your partner. Be the change you wish to see, as Gandhi said. Falling in love all over again, with your husband, wife, or partner is a re-kindling of the love that has always been there, on the back burner. It is time to turn the gas up, on the burner all the way, to sizzle. Move out of mediocrity and into scintillating. Dress up for your partner and stay at home, instead of going out for dinner. Romantic dinners at home are best, because you don't have to drive afterward. You can take each other's clothes off before you begin eating dessert. Maybe you will be the main course!

Any relationship can last short-term. Chemistry does not make a lasting relationship—chemistry is just the beginning. Expanding that chemistry into a profound connection of mind-body-spirit passion has the power to last and is the key to creating the ultimate relationship.

As my friend William Dargin II says, "Keep your hands and feet inside of the vehicle, and fasten your seatbelts! Let go and enjoy the ride, because life is just one big ORGASM!"

Sea of Yesterdays

Will you join me in this blissful state?
Will you join me in my Joy?
Will you hold me when I'm feeling pain?
Will you let me be the boy?
Will you love me when I'm hateful?
Will you love me when I'm not?
You loved me when I was 'beauty
Will you love me when I'm not?
Will you join me on this journey?
Will you stay with me this night?
Will you love me as I am, my dear?
Will you help me feel tonight?
Will you join me on this journey?
While we create this day
Will you have me in the morning?
While I beg for you to stay
My love for you is endless
It stands the test of time
For we only are beginning

To go beyond the rhyme

Can you be mine forever
As any can I know
It takes a sea of yesterdays
To see without the woe
Our lives it seems do change and bond
Our souls upon this plane
We live our lives in separate ways
Until the end of days

Will you walk this road with me?
Until I walk no more
Will you be the candle for me
When I go upon shore?

Jennifer Elizabeth Masters
May 13, 2014

About The Author

Jennifer Elizabeth Masters is a hypnotherapist, Master energy healer, certified life, love, sex coach and gifted intuitive. But above all, Jennifer is just a mother and a woman. As an adventurer of life, it has been one careening roller coaster ride, which has brought such wondrous thrills, squeals, and delights.

Life is what you make it. Jennifer has certainly made hers one of joy, love, and inspiration to her clients, friends, and family. Her glass is over-flowing, rather than half-empty. Life can always get better—we only have to ask for it to be so.

Living authentically, fully, and joyfully is the gift that Jennifer shares with workshop attendees and clients. As a pathfinder, she assists others to find theirs, empowering, and uplifting through guidance and wisdom. Jennifer's education has been on the road of life. She shares what she has learned with transparency, without fear.

Jennifer offers workshops, retreats, and private

sessions.

India, Bali, Costa Rica, Australia and the UK are all on her list of upcoming events.

Her website is **JenniferElizabethMasters.com**

You can e-mail her at:

JenniferElizabethMasters@gmail.com

Additional Resources

Jennifer's Website:
www.JenniferElizabethMasters.com

1. *Odyssey Victim to Victory* by Jennifer Elizabeth Masters

2. *Shake Your Soul Song* by Devi Ward

3. *The Guide to Getting It On* by Paul Joannides

4. *She Comes First: The Thinking Man's Guide to Pleasuring A Woman* by Ian Kerner

5. *He Comes Next: The Thinking Woman's Guide to Pleasuring a Man* by Ian Kerner

6. *Vagina, A Cultural History* Naomi Wolf

7. *The Elusive Orgasm* by Vivienne Cass

8. *Sex Positions You Never Thought Possible* by JAIYA

9. The Science of Orgasm, by Komisaruk, Beyer-Flores and Whipple, (2006)

10. *Communication Miracles for Couples: Easy and Effective Tools to Create More Love and Less Conflict* by Jonathan

Robinson

11. *The Science of Kissing: What Our Lips Are Telling Us* by Sheril Kirshenbaum

12. www.MyLabsForLife.com – Excellent advice, lab work and natural health coaching for hormone, etc

www.ingramcontent.com/pod-product-compliance
Lightning Source LLC
Chambersburg PA
CBHW070025100426
42740CB00013B/2598